Please remember you are seen,
known and loved!

Jhe C Agamah

What People Are Saying
about Caryl's Closet

"In *Caryl's Closet*, June Wood Agamah truly paints pictures with words in her colorful descriptions of growing up in a small village in Guyana, South America. Reading about the unique challenges she faced as an immigrant to America opened my eyes to see how much I take for granted in my own life. In spite of many difficulties and struggles, June's strong faith in God shines like a golden thread woven through her memoir, giving her joy and strength, wisdom and grace. This book will certainly be a treasure to her three beautiful daughters and generations to come."

—POLLY DANFORTH

"In many ways, your story evokes empathy. A few examples would be through the weaving of your dad's story into your story and within the incredible odds you faced together. Whether it was seen in his incredible work ethic, within his family, or within the relationship he had with your mother, his story exemplifies grit and perseverance. I also found it encouraging for you to be able to witness the transformation that your father went through as your children entered the scene. It was an admirable and visible softening of his heart.

"I was also able to see the love your mother and father displayed and how it translated and affected your own life, in positive ways. You continue to look for the good, even throughout the ups and the downs of life. And you grew from it. In doing so, you allowed your children to live vicariously through your stories and experiences. So much so, it is as if they were able to experience it firsthand.

"It is obvious, through the writing of this book, just how important it was to each of your children to learn more about you and their history. It is a testimony of their consistent fascination to know more about you and your family history, and in turn, more about themselves."

—"A Friend in Christ"

"The highlights of the book for me were your stories about your mother and father, the way you celebrated holidays, village traditions in Buxton, etc. I dog-eared several pages with well-written descriptive paragraphs that really put me in the situation."

—Lucy Lackie

"June's writings will open your senses to the sights, sounds, and tastes of her unique experiences. She will take you with her on a journey that crosses states, countries, and continents, all the while pointing you to the One who created it all."

—Claudia Kirby

"Our good friend June shares her story about coming to America and finding Home."

—Jim Pickett, Retired Aircraft Industry Executive

"June Agamah opens her heart to us in this story of her life. She shares her journey with honesty and insight as she discovers who she is and her purpose in this world."

—Dianne Poe Pickett, Retired Educator

"When I listen to June read the words of her new book aloud, I feel transported to Guyana and can almost touch and smell the rich culture through June's soothing and descriptive language! I can't wait to pick up this book and be taken to South America and learn about the people and places that shaped my dear friend, June."

—Dr. Hannah Brooks

"Interesting story that features a country few know anything about. The reader gets to follow June as she comes of age, from Guyana to Barbados, then to America in her journey as an immigrant."

—John Simpson

"Firstly, thank you for allowing me to be part of this journey with you. I feel as though I have been all over the world. Truly, your story is going to touch many hearts. You brought me to tears many times and I know people will connect with your life, your love, and your faith through the genuine artful way you shared it with your words.

"You are a beautiful writer. I could see how you fully fit yourself inside your own narrative about a quarter of the way through. Thank you for sharing this with the world. It is too important not to."

—Tiarra Tompkins

"As 2020 has been a year of unprecedented uncertainty, COVID-19, unrest, and controversy, *Caryl's Closet* is an uplifting, welcome source of hope in troubled times. She reminds us to find opportunity in challenges, faith in despair, and to remember our humanity—our connections—as we find strength in one another. *Caryl's Closet* is a joyous, inspirational testimony to all that we can accomplish . . . *together!*"

—GAIL FALLEN, EDITOR; TALK SHOW HOST,
1310 KFKA, 1310KFKA.COM

Caryl's Closet

Caryl's Closet

A journey of faith and
love which starterd in a
village in Guyana and went
around the world.

by
June Wood Agamah

Carpenter's Son Publishing

Published by Carpenter's Son Publishing, Franklin, Tennessee

Published in association with Larry Carpenter of
Christian Book Services, LLC
www.christianbookservices.com

Scripture is used from the The Holy Bible, Today's New International Version® unless otherwise noted. Copyright © 2001, 2005 by Biblica®. Used by permission of Biblica®. All rights reserved worldwide.

Edited by Tiarra Tompkins

Proofread by Gail Fallen

Cover and Interior Layout Design by Suzanne Lawing

Printed in the United States of America

978-1-952025-39-6

To my husband, Edem,
And my three daughters,
Sarah, Aseye, and Miriam:
The loves of my life.

With every action, there is an equal response to what you put out. I choose to put out love. Love has never failed me. It is the most powerful force on earth. Love can scale walls, climb mountains, and walk through valleys. Let your love shine so that others could give glory to the God who placed you on this earth to be a difference maker.

—June Wood Agamah

Contents

Foreword

> *Never be afraid to trust an unknown*
> *future to a known God.*
> —Corrie ten Boom

June Caryl Wood Agamah, a Guyanese immigrant, felt like she had finally achieved success and her American dream . . . but at a price. Her daughters do not know who she is.

In *Caryl's Closet,* June Caryl takes us on a journey as she comes of age and seeks to unearth her thoughts that she carried in journals over the years. Her quest is thwarted by circumstances beyond her control, but she must rely on her childhood upbringing and the lessons learned from her slave ancestors to forge a path through immigration struggles from a tiny village, Buxton-Friendship in Guyana, South America; to Barbados; and finally, to the United States of America.

Her dad, Howell, was a pioneer. Despite leaving school at the age of 14 to support his family, he instilled in June a desire to learn. He built their new home from the ground up with help from friends, while riding 24 miles to work and back, five days a week. He raised hogs, chickens, and ducks and tended a large garden to supplement his family income. His hard work provided the example June needed when it was time for her to start her own journey.

June Caryl provides us with the heart-warming and sometimes heartbreaking challenges the villagers and her family faced in order to rise above the lingering effects of slavery. Her village, Buxton-Friendship, where "Education was King," became famously known for "Buxton People Stop Train." She provides descriptive details of celebratory events in her village and how members of her community rallied around each other to allow members of her small community to excel.

Life in Guyana took a turn for the worse after her father, Howell, lost his job and the political landscape in the country changed. The government was experimenting with a new way of life, moving from being a democratically run state to a republic. Socialism was the new order of the time.

Her father and his family needed to seek greener pastures. He, his wife, and youngest daughter sought refuge in America. Immigration laws prevented June Caryl from accompanying her family. At 21 years of age, she was no longer a minor. She was left to fend for herself and sought opportunities to work in Barbados.

One of the things I love about this book is the detailed description of scenes from her childhood memories. These memories take me way back. Memories of which I am keenly aware of, since I too am a Guyanese transplant. I caught up with "Caryl" during her sojourn in search for new adventure in Barbados.

We were hosted by the same family, briefly, with some mutual friends when she arrived in Barbados, but for different reasons, we went our separate ways on the island. After my conversion to Christ, I reconnected with her and sought to encourage her to do the same by visiting her often. I shared my delight in gospel music and enthusiasm about my newly found faith in Christ with Caryl. We lost contact during the summer of 1983. After I migrated to America in 1996, we reconnected in 1998. I was excited to learn that the gospel seed the Lord used me to sow in June in Barbados was not in vain. June Caryl, at some stage in her sojourn to America, had turned her life over to Jesus Christ. June Caryl's story reaches to the heart of each of us. It strips away at the core of nuanced behaviors and expectations. She is brutality honest about her struggles to survive as an immigrant. A common hustle, all too familiar to immigrants with all of its clumsiness. Her voice in her climb to success is palpable.

June Caryl shares the difference she experienced between knowing about a God and knowing Him personally. Through her struggles to navigate the immigration systems of Barbados to the United States and inside the heart-stopping reality of loss when she lost her mom when her parents first migrated to the struggles she and her father endured to make ends meet in New Orleans, Louisiana, *Caryl's Closet* details her determination to educate herself, a tradition birthed from her freed slave ancestors to lift themselves out of poverty. Her story gives us an intimate look at how immigrants navigate the American system to make a better life for themselves.

This journey demonstrates that without faith, hard work, sacrifice, and determination, life is daunting. In her struggles to find her footing, she realized that she could not do so on her own strength. June Caryl had to rely on the One who sees and knows her.

Caryl's Closet provides genuine insight into the vivid emotional struggles June Caryl experienced with her father when she decided to marry someone outside of their Guyanese culture. These scenes are familiar to the average immigrant, and I find myself reflecting on my own journey as an immigrant in search of love.

Many stories can feel as though you have heard them before. This book is not one of those stories. This book is a page turner, and when she gave me the opportunity to read it prior to print, I was not only honored but I also couldn't put the book down. I wanted to know what happened next as she ventured into amazing unknown adventures. I felt carried along with June Caryl's search for relevance as an immigrant in a society that's filled with roadblocks that many immigrants face when they choose to leave their home for a journey into something and somewhere new.

This book is narrated with grace and honesty. You are taken along as June Caryl distills each scene and event with purposeful clarity. I was encouraged by her faithful determination and resilience as she is able to thrive in the predominantly White spaces during her journey in America. It is a lesson to all of us. When you have God on your side, you can conquer all that you encounter. I hope you enjoy reading this book like I did.

—NORRIS HENRY, SENIOR PASTOR,
BREAKING BARRIERS MINISTRIES BOWIE

Preface

*Our destiny rest in our own hands! You're the author
of your own life story; therefore, act it well so
that you'll have no regrets!*
—ANONYMOUS

Have you ever spent so long seeking to accomplish a dream
that you almost forget who you are and where you came from?
My old journals in hand, my daughter, Aseye, confronted me
about who I was. It was in that moment that I had to come to
grips with my story. Her need to know our history and heritage made me realize that my voice matters in telling my story.
It is about a journey through which others could benefit by
unearthing their stories also.

Caryl's Closet is a "framed memoir." My story chronicles
my journey from Guyana to Barbados to America while using
flashbacks and memories to piece together the front story of
what's happening as I figure out the truth of who I really am.

I'm a writer. I had forgotten how much I love to write. I
have always needed to write, but I had shoved that desire on
the back burner in order to fulfill my desire to be educated,

to lift myself out of poverty. My goal was to accomplish the American Dream.

Each life journey, each story, comes with lessons and themes that we can all relate to. It is our shared humanity that connects us. My story's theme is not only a coming-of-age journey through life, culture, and faith, it is also a gift to my readers: something heartfelt, sometimes hilarious, and every bit of it true.

Prologue

The greatest task of anyone is to find meaning in his or her life. Suffering in and of itself is meaningless.
—Viktor Frankl in *Man's Search for Meaning*

I was born in obscurity. I don't know how much I weighed. I never had my baby picture taken. My parents were too poor and busy trying to make ends meet to capture these mementos of the beginning of my story.

Despite the circumstances surrounding my birth, I do not believe in such a thing as random moments or situations. I do believe we are put on this earth to work out our individual purpose, and when we find it and walk in it, we are successful. Truth be told, that's what I thought the American Dream was all about. So many of us spend all our time looking behind that we miss what is ahead. Have you ever spent too long staring into your past? I believed in ignoring what was behind; don't dwell on the past, forge ahead; put your head down and work hard! Isn't that what all immigrants do? It's precisely what my aunt and uncle, who came to the US before my mom and dad, did. It's what my parents did and that's what I did. I expected my three American-born daughters to do the same. Little did I know how blind I was.

Most immigrant parents live by the paradigms they know. My worldview began to shift in the summer of 2014, with one conversation with my middle daughter, Aseye. Similar interactions followed and resulted in the change of my whole perspective on life. These exchanges helped unearth the many hidden and forgotten gems of my life. She showed me that by suppressing my past, I was hiding away the richness of my story.

It was my birthday in June and my family gathered to celebrate me. My middle daughter, Aseye, had secretly rummaged through my old, worn photo albums to look for my baby pictures. To her dismay, there were none. However, she found what she calls "these treasures." As she is the writer in the family, we gathered around her laptop to see what she had created for my birthday. As a present to me, she had created a picture blog of my photos taken in the 1980s that she had discovered hidden in my closet. Despite spending so long determined not to look back, I was overjoyed and burst into tears. Later, she confessed that this project was also for her search and discovery of her identity. Aseye was looking for building blocks to stand on. She had so many questions about who her parents were and who she was becoming.[1]

---

1. Aseye Agamah, "Caryl's Closet: An Ode to My Mother and Her Style in the 1980s," *Aseye Says* (blog), December 29, 2014, https://aseyesays.wordpress.com/2014/12/29/caryls-closet-an-ode-to-my-mother-and-her-style-in-the-1980s/.

Then she asked, "Mom, what did you look like as a child? How about in grade school? You grew up in a village, right? What was that like?"

Her questions came faster than I could answer, and I fumbled for words to explain why I had consciously or unconsciously blocked most of my past. Many of us face things behind us that we may not have been ready to process.

For me, I had found that pain is a teacher. Pain forces one to work, love, and find courage during difficult times. Pain is also uncomfortable and unpleasant, so once those times were over it was best to forget. I had stuffed everything about my past life in a closet and nailed the door shut!

After our conversation, I could see the importance in my daughter's eyes to understand where we came from. To understand our culture. I took baby steps to showcase my past by sending my daughters the Buxton-Friendship Online and Guyanese Online magazines to read about my village. These magazines have features about life in my village and Guyanese people in America who have made great contributions in academia, music, movies, and the arts.[2] Every time I came across important tidbits about Guyana, I brought them to my daughters' awareness. I thought that was enough to quell the desire for information about their mother's past life in Guyana.

Four years ago, before I began writing this memoir, was the day of my reckoning. I was relaxing in my bedroom when it literally came as a knock on my door.

"Who is it?" I asked.

---

2. Buxton-Friendship *Express*, August 2019, Buxton Guyana, http://buxtonguyana.net/Buxton-FriendshipExpress2019-08.pdf.

"It's me, Mom."

It was Aseye.

"Come on in. What are you up to now?" I asked.

I had a smile in my voice, but Aseye appeared pensive and very businesslike. She was cradling a set of journals in her arm. As she got closer to me, she threw them on the bed next to me.

"What are these?" she asked.

At first, I did not recognize them. Then like a tsunami, the memories flooded my mind! I could barely form words.

"Where did you get those from?"

"I found them in your closet!" Aseye exclaimed.

Despite her knowing my stand on letting the past go, I couldn't help but see the excitement and the inexhaustible amount of questions she had swirling in her eyes. I had traversed oceans, cities, towns, and subdivisions with my thoughts loaded in those journals. However, I had laid them down to finally rest in my closet! I didn't think I would be sitting here, preparing to relive these moments again.

She pushed me over and sat next to me.

"Look, Mom, you even met one of my favorite authors, James Baldwin!" She sighed. "Mom, you don't even know how much finding these mean to. . . ."

Her voice cracked and trailed off. Then she looked me full in my face.

"Mom, you are a writer. Please, Mom, look at these!"

I had moved so many times. Worn pages and faded ink told stories of places I had been; oceans traversed, cities, towns and subdivisions lived in and left. These journals were the culmination of my thoughts. Along the way, I had lost touch with who I was because I had hidden parts of my past away. That is when I decided to write my story.

This book, *Caryl's Closet*, will take you on a ride where no one else has ever been.[3] It is my story. It's a story of me, a young Guyanese girl, coming of age in a changing society. My story is set amidst the backdrop of a new political system that threatened the Guyanese way of life and the village where I was born. It further unfolds as I grapple with the immigration systems of Guyana and Barbados. I invite you to please follow me on my journey to the United States. Accompany me, as I maneuver the intricate maze through which immigrants navigate the American system to make a better life for themselves. Look with me inside the heart-stopping reality of loss and the struggles that my father and I endured to make ends meet in New Orleans, Louisiana. Walk with me on my journey to educate myself. You see, education was a valued tradition from my freed slave ancestors, to lift oneself out of poverty.

In this book, I paint pictures in words of each scene, because I do not have pictures to show you. I only have words. I only have the ability to connect with others through forgiveness, gratitude, kindness, grace, and love. And that, I find, is the answer to life's purpose for me. I want to pass on these traits to others in my sphere of influence. Connecting with others has always been important to me. My mother, Walterine, demonstrated that by the way she lived during her short life on earth.

I want you, my readers, to feel what I felt. I hope that you can see through my eyes. I want you to encounter with me the faith and resilience that it takes to navigate the predominantly

---

3. Agamah, *Aseye Says* (blog), "Ode to My Mother."

White spaces I traversed during my journey. My hope is that through my story, readers can look at immigrants with new eyes. When the world tries to keep us in its mold, we too can break out with the unvarnished truth that unconditional love will always prevail in the end.

With this book, I want to unpack my closet. I want my children to know that I did have a life! We, as immigrants, leave everything that was dear to us. We hoped for and moved toward a "better life." We made sacrifices, but we forget to live in the present. Now we must remember to share our stories to connect our children with our past. We must let them know that our past influences the fabric of their lives. I've learned that when our children discover these treasures, it contributes to them feeling connected and whole.

I hope my story reminds you to think of your own unearthed treasures that are the stories of your life.

Introduction

Perhaps the turning point in one's life is realizing that to be treated like a victim is not necessarily to become one.
—JAMES BALDWIN: ON VICTIMHOOD

How do you measure life? Is it measured by the way we live, serve, and give? Or should life be measured by the words we say, the love we express through a hug or smile, or the kindness we share with others? As a young person, those were the deep questions I had.

Whenever anyone would ask me what I wanted to be when I grew up, I would be honest and say, "I don't know." They would press on and ask, "What about becoming a teacher? How about a nurse?" I was ambitious, and I studied very hard and got good grades in school. In high school, I was good in several sports and of all my classes loved physics the most, because I liked the way my teacher took us outside the physics lab and demonstrated things using nature.

My best girlfriend and I loved reading. To prove it, we joined the Buxton-Friendship Village Library and were determined to read every book on the shelf before we graduated from secondary school. I read most of the Nancy Drew and Hardy Boys books. Books about the Barbary pirates, biographies, and historical novels were also interesting to read. Later in my teens, I read *To Kill a Mockingbird*. It remains one of my favorite books, ever. I also love reading Jane Austen's works such as *Pride and Prejudice, Persuasion, Emma,* and *Sense and Sensibility*. My favorite stories are those in which a person of character decides to go against the grain and does what is right regardless of the consequences. I also love books in which the author uses descriptions that make the reader feel like they are right there to experience the scenes. It helps the reader identify with the protagonist.

Even though I was surrounded by talented and successful people, after graduating from high school in 1977, I struggled to find my footing. There were no high school career counselors, no mentors at home to give clarity to my pathway. Neither of my parents had graduated from high school, much less traveled the road through the rigors of academics that might lead me to productive work in civic life. As many of us who go against the grain, I had to find my own wings to fly.

In the summer of 1982, I moved to Barbados, in the West Indies. I had hopes that I could create a life there. My hopes of landing a promising career were dashed. There, I worked for a professional family as their nanny and housekeeper. I share about the magnificent beauty of the island and the rhythms of life in what is known as "Little England."[4]

---

4. Jane Shattuck Hoyos, "Why Barbados is Called 'Little England,'" *Planet Barbados* (blog), February 15, 2010, http://planetbarbadosblog.com/2010/02/why-barbados-is-called-little-england/.

A phone call from my Cousin Eunice, from Slidell, Louisiana, led me on another journey: my family needed me to get to America immediately!

I eventually had to return to Guyana, South America, to pick up my green card.

After my return from Guyana, I officially received permanent resident status in the United States of America in 1984. I enrolled in the University of New Orleans in 1985, and during my final year, I met and married my husband, Edem. We moved to Evanston, Illinois, in 1991, then to Chicago, Illinois, in 1993. I landed a job with Aurora University, a private liberal arts college located in Aurora, Illinois, for three years. As assistant to the dean of student services, I acted as a liaison between Aurora University and the Illinois Masonic Medical Center RN and the bachelor's degree nursing program.

We left Chicago, three kids in tow, and moved to Springfield, Illinois, in 1995. I was determined to keep educating myself. I attended graduate school at night, at the University of Illinois at Springfield. Edem would watch the girls while I went to school. I earned my master's in public health (MPH) in 2001. For the past 25 years, my family and I have lived in Springfield, Illinois.

Throughout my journey, from Guyana, South America; to Barbados, West Indies; the United States; and the country of Ghana, West Africa, I have experienced grief, loneliness, rejection, and discrimination. Yet, I was filled with determination. I have heard the voice of God clearly and experienced God's abiding love. I learned the importance of daring to be the "outlier"[5] in order to be in God's perfect will.

5. Artharva Sangle, "How You Can Outlie the Norm," *Noteworthy–The Journal* (blog), May 12, 2019, https://blog.usejournal.com/how-can-you-outlie-the-norm-362dcbb66568.

Since 1996, I have worked extensively in the public health arena, both in Sangamon County and abroad. I worked briefly as visiting online coordinator for the University of Illinois at Springfield, Illinois, from September 2017 to September 2018. I have also had the opportunity to serve on a few nonprofit boards.

In October 2014, I was recognized by the University of Illinois as the winner of the Humanitarian Award for my work as an international healthcare advocate, organizer, and educator.

In April 2015, my husband and I were awarded the *State Journal-Registrar* Finalist for the First Citizen and Legacy Award in Healthcare for our work in Ghana, West Africa.

I have gained extensive experience working with a diverse group of people over the years and understand the importance of working together to accomplish the core functions of public health—assessment, policy development, and assurance.

Over the past 20 years, I hope I have made a difference in the lives of many people in the United States; Guyana, South America; and Ghana, West Africa. I have made great sacrifices throughout my life. My father, Howell Wood, lived a life of hard work and self-reliance. At the age of 59 years, he risked everything in order to make a better life for his family. Though impoverished, he journeyed from living in a two-bedroom house in Guyana, South America, to come to America. Providing adequately for his family will always be his legacy. My mother, Walterine, taught me and modeled how to serve and love others unconditionally.

These family character traits of hard work, enduring faith, long-suffering determination, and perseverance were dug deep and rooted in me. I chose to pass on these family traits to our three daughters—the soon-to-be Dr. Akpene Agamah, Ms. Aseye Agamah, and the soon-to-be Dr. Alikem Agamah—and to future generations to come.

I share all of these to show you how much you can do if you are willing to work hard and rely on the inner fierce determination that we all have. It doesn't matter where you come from or where you go. God will bring you through the journey of creating incredible stories that become part of your legacy when you follow Him, and you serve and love.

1.

Family Life in Buxton–
Friendship Village Then

*Success is to be measured not so much by the position
that one has reached in life as by the obstacles which
he/she has overcome while trying to succeed.*
—BOOKER T. WASHINGTON

Every morning, rain or shine, my mother would get up at the
crack of dawn to help my dad get ready for work. Work was 12
miles away in Georgetown, the capital of Guyana. She would
boil the water for his Thermos flask and pack his lunch pail
while he pumped air in the bicycle tires for the journey. He
would work all day as a carpenter and ride back home before
it got too dark.

In a tiny village, Friendship-Buxton, I was the last of five
children to be born (until a decade later when my youngest
sister was born in early 1960) in Guyana, South America.
When I was born, my father was elated about my birth because everything was going well with his job and he was in
a happy place. He had been promoted that year to head up

the Guyana Sea Defense Project to help prevent the Atlantic Ocean from flooding the residential areas along the east coast of Demerara, Guyana. For our family, life was bearable.

My dad had a remarkable retentive memory. We were too poor and could not afford to go to "town." Our visions of Georgetown and Guyana in all its glory were limited to the stories our dad would tell us about how clean and beautiful the streets and the famous botanical gardens were. He would tell us how easy it was to get lost if one did not have a good memory to remember where you were going and where you just came from. My sister Ingrid and I were eventually able to experience life in beautiful Georgetown during our teenage years. Knowing that my father had to leave school at the age of 14 to work at the sugar estate in Mon Repos to help his mother take care of his other siblings gave us perspective to his intelligence as we grew. Even without the education from traditional school, my dad still worked hard and later studied carpentry under the guidance of a skilled carpenter in the village.

Our old shingle shack consisted of a dining room/half kitchen area and one bedroom. The kitchen was detached from the house and we, all seven of us, had to use an outhouse and a bathroom to clean ourselves. Mom and Dad slept on the bed, and my sister and I slept on mats on the floor in the bedroom while our brothers slept on the floor of the dining room.

My mom did her best to make our home a beautiful place. She loved beautiful things, and she would use that love and her creativity to take our shack and create a space that showed that love. She repurposed magazines of beautiful women, places, and buildings as wallpaper. She used glue from the Glamar cherry tree in our front yard, adding water to paste these images on the walls of our dining room area (like wallpaper that's used today). This created a comforting, airy feel. I used to gaze at the lovely contours of females dressed in colorful Asian attire, their tiny heads graced with wide-brimmed hats.

Alternatively, I would marvel at the dazzling shapes and colors juxtaposed on the African cloth worn by every tone of black- and brown-skinned ladies. On the center of every table laid my mother's signature duck-shaped crocheted centerpieces. And in every vase were the artificial flowers she created with colorful waxed paper to form an array of petals, shaped like narrow tulips and wide or tiny roses. Each stem was created by wrapping green felt or paper around sturdy pieces of cut wires. The room held a wooden dining room table with enough room to sit a family of eight. There was a window separating the dining area from a small kitchen-like space for my mom to store her groceries and a small kerosene stove. Our home was small, but sitting on the sofa in our living room, one tended to forget that our home was an old shingle shack on the outside. Instead, it felt like home, a welcoming place to be.

In America, we tend to hear "high-school dropout" and attach to it a negative assumption about the person. Despite this title fitting my mom, it didn't define who she was. She was creative in many ways. Even though she had my oldest brother when she was just a teenager, she still worked hard. She started off working for wealthy families inside their homes. Once my older siblings came along, she worked from home. She gave birth to five children within a span of 10 years while still supplementing the family's income by washing clothing for wealthy people in the village.

Have you ever taken for granted some of the most simple of things? Washing clothes now is a cinch; it takes two minutes to set up the washing machine and walk away to return to clean clothes ready to be put in the dryer. My mom washed clothing by hand. Then she starched and hand ironed them. For many years, she ironed using a "coal pot" iron. She would fill the chamber of the iron with charcoal and then light it through the holes on the sides with a long match. Next, she'd wipe off the soot and iron the shirts, dresses, and trousers until they were crisp.

When the "flat iron" came into vogue, Mom used it in her work. She would heat the iron on her propane stove. She would use thick pieces of old cloth to pick up the hot iron by its handle and complete her work in less time than it took to iron with the coal pot iron.

We had a daily routine. Every morning, we'd roll up our sleeping mats and hang them outside on the wooden fence to "sun." Whenever it rained, we had to be vigilant to grab our mats and take them inside. I had my first lesson in "Economics 101" from my mother. Each person had his or her own enamelware plate, cup, and spoon. The plates and cups were colorful. Some were patterned and others were plain colored. Some that fell on the floor wore their dents to serve another day. My mother would plan the weekly menu so we all knew what foods to expect each day of the week. At mealtime, the table was set and each person knew where to sit. Prayers were said before every meal. One hung on our wall and I still remember that prayer. *Be present at our table, Lord, for each and every meal. May creatures bless and grant that we may feast in paradise with thee. Amen.* As a child, I wondered who the "creatures" were but never asked. I was too afraid to ask. Instead, I would conjure up thoughts of crawly bugs and lizards.

Years later, in the summer of 2017, my husband and our three children accompanied our friend to her homeland,

Flam, in Norway. As we visited several bookstores and gift shops, I noticed several versions of that prayer and discovered that it is a Norwegian prayer and hymn. So how did a Norwegian prayer find its way into the tiny home of mine in Guyana, South America? Further probing of the history of Guyana revealed that in the 1950s, Guyana was one of several overseas territories from which 82 percent of British Guiana bauxite was procured and shipped to Norway.[6]

The gold-printed words read, *Christ is the head of this house, the unseen guest at every meal, the silent listener to every conversation.*

My older sister and I sometimes wondered if Christ was waiting to catch us when we secretly exchanged food on Sundays. You see, in our home, there was no such thing as "choice" in the Wood family vocabulary. Whatever my mother put on our plates, that's what we ate, period! So the challenge for my sister and me was how to seamlessly make the exchange of meals. She hated split peas soup and I hated "metemgee," (a combination of yams, plantains, eddoes, cassava, okra, and other vegetables, boiled together with salted fish and coconut milk).[7] So one of us sacrificed going hungry for the other to avoid a spanking for not eating. When my parents weren't looking, we took turns eating for the other.

6. United States Economic Cooperation Administration Public Advisory Board, Report for the Public Advisory Board of the Economic Cooperation Administration, Volume 37, https://www.google.com/books/edition/Report_for_the_Public_Advisory_Board_of/nmkUAAAAIAAJ?hl=en&gb-pv=1&dq=inauthor:%22United+States.+Economic+Cooperation+Administration%22&printsec=frontcover.
7. "Guyanese Metemgee," Jehan Can Cook, January 26, 2020, http://jehancancook.com/2020/01/guyanese-metemgee/.

For the longest time, I was the baby in the family. Not only was I the youngest, but I was a girl child among three older brothers. Legend has it that, like most men, our dad wanted his firstborn child to be a boy. His wishes were met when Lennox was born. He yearned for a girl next. But their second child was a boy, Rudolph. One would think that the "third time is a charm," like they say. Not in this case. They tried for a girl again and they got another boy, Elroy. Finally, on the fourth try, my sister Ingrid was born. I was their fifth child. Ten years later, my sister Nola was born. So the Wood family was complete with three boys and three girls.

The surprising fact is that my mom attended the St. Augustine's Anglican Church regularly while my dad insisted on attending the Methodist church. Despite being split between two separate churches, my sister Ingrid and I attended the Anglican church with our mom, but we were confirmed in the Methodist church. My oldest brother, Lennox, attended the Anglican church but I do not recall ever seeing my brothers Rudolph and Elroy in church.

Your world is what you make it. I was generally a happy-go-lucky kid, and I enjoyed school and play. We were allowed to go home from school for lunch and then return for the afternoon session. I could not wait for the school bell to ring, and I would be so thrilled that it was lunch time! Then, suddenly, I would get to a certain distance from my home and that familiar smell would waft through the air and hit my nose. It was Tuesday! Boy, how I hated Tuesdays! That's when Mom served the dreaded metemgee. My emotions would turn from joy to anger. I would stop dead in my tracks. I would start crying. I cried in my mom's Economics 101 class because every Wood child was expected to eat everything on his or her plate or go hungry the rest of the day until dinnertime! Tuesdays were the worst days of my life!

There was another recourse for my sister and me. Since my parents were very industrious, our yard was full of fruit trees. We found creative ways to survive the "eat everything" rule. The Buxton Spice Mango is named after our village.[8] It is arguably one of the sweetest mangoes in the world. It is fleshy and sweet with a unique spicy taste. During "mango" season, our brothers would pick and bring home large bags of mangoes. They would hide the mangoes in a dark place, under dried reed grass, which aided in ripening the mangoes. Each day, we would check for ripe mangoes and eat them for breakfast, lunch, and dinner.

Since Guyana is a tropical country, fruits are left on the tree or vine to ripen. Our mid-sized yard (two plots of land) was outlined with fruit trees. We ate fruits in a variety of ways. We picked cherries and added sugar to them; we also picked ripened tamarinds, added sugar, pepper, and salt, and molded them into round balls. We would peel golden apples and mix the pieces with salt and pepper. We mixed soursop with condensed milk and sugar. We ate bananas, guavas, sapodillas, pineapples, star apples, and gooseberries. We made lemonade from limes and lemons and made pineapple drinks by soaking pineapple skin, sugar, clove, and cinnamon overnight to create a refreshing drink. We picked sorrel, dried the leaves, and created a sorrel drink. Maube, a drink made from the bark of a tree, with a touch of bitter and sweet flavor, is still a favor-

---

8. A Google search for "Buxton Spice Mango" generated nearly 160,000 results.

ite of most Guyanese today. We picked green plantains, sliced them thinly, and fried them in vegetable oil to make fried plantains. We would let the plantains ripen until the skin was yellowish-brown, then fry them in hot oil. This smorgasbord of fruits and homemade snacks kept us satiated. Although we were poor, we never went hungry a day of my life!

Being the youngest sibling for so many years had its pros and cons. Everyone doted on me, but I still remember being teased relentlessly by my bothers. One summer, I was playing outside with my chicken friends. I don't remember where my brothers found this snake. Maybe they brought it home from working on the farm in the backlands of our village. Unbeknownst to me, the snake was dead. When I heard my brothers had returned, I ran to meet them as usual. They told me they had brought a pet for me. I looked inside the basket, and there it was. A grayish-white snake. I took one look at it lying there, jumped back, and started running toward the back of our yard. I was screaming for help. I did not get very far, because my brothers were standing at strategic ends of the house, surrounding me. They would throw the dead snake from one brother to the other. So everywhere I turned, my path was being blocked. I felt my heart pounding in my chest. The last thing I remembered were the sounds of laughter and the sight of my middle brother Rudolph grinning from ear to ear. My feet buckled under me and I passed out!

Division of Labor

Each member of our family was assigned his or her job. My brothers did most of the "outside" work. Any heavy lifting or climbing jobs were designated to the boys in the family. They were responsible for taking out the garbage; feeding the pigs and other domestic animals; and watering the plants and harvesting the fruits during the ripened season for the genips, dunks, bananas, plantain, coconut, mangoes, and other fruits.[9] We all helped with watering of the vegetable garden and other plants. I loved to feed the chickens and gather the white or brown eggs. I knew each chicken by name and would speak to them. They became my friends.

Part of my responsibility as a female child was to wash the dishes in the sink in the detached kitchen. I would gather the dishes, then walk carefully down four steps leading down from the house into the kitchen. Most of the time, it took me two to three trips back and forth depending on the number of dishes to be washed. I still remember having to walk a mile to and from our home to fetch water when the pipeline broke and water was temporarily unavailable from the pipes in our yard. I truly had the "When I was a kid, I had to walk a mile to get water!" stories! I had to use two large enamel bowls. One bowl was for washing the dishes with soapy water and the other had "fresh" water to rinse the dishes.

Then I would leave the dishes to "drain" on a makeshift wooden dish rack made by my dad.

Washing the pots and pans was the hardest part of the job for me. These pots and pans were made from steel mixed with aluminum and were hard for me to lift. Sometimes, remnants from the cook-up rice dish (called the "bun bun") would be too hard for my little hands to pry or dig out, so I had to leave the utensil to "soak" overnight or call on my older siblings to help me. I don't know why, but for me there was something

---

9. A Google search for "Buxton Spice Mango" generated nearly 160,000 results.

cathartic about doing the dishes. Often, I belted out familiar Sunday school songs as loudly as my little voice could project. Our next-door neighbors became accustomed to this ritual and often spurred me on by joining in with the chorus.

If you have siblings, you know that accidents happen. Working in proximity can be detrimental to a large family. So innocent mistakes occurred.

One evening, around six o'clock, I was leaving the outdoor kitchen to climb the steps to our house. I suddenly felt a stinging sensation on my left leg. I yelled, grabbed my left foot, and jumped around in a circular motion. I heard heavy footsteps darting down the stairs and I was lifted off the ground. It was my big brother carrying me. I didn't know it at the time, but he had just boiled some water on the stove and wanted to dispose of the excess water in the pot, so he threw it outdoors. My left leg still carries that mark to this day. I was in the right place at the wrong time!

We were fortunate to own two plots of land, thus my family always raised cats, dogs, and pigs. I loved taking care of the little kittens and the piglets. I remember once, the mother cat had just given birth to four baby kittens. I would spend hours sitting cross-legged on the dining room floor watching them suck milk from their mom's breasts. Then one day, the unthinkable happened. Someone (to this day I cannot remember who), pulled out a dresser drawer too far. The mother cat was nursing her young below and the drawer fell and hit the cat family. The mother cat escaped. I screamed and yelled for my mother to come see. Two of my beautiful kitties were gone! I stared in horror at the damage, and for months I could not get that image out of my head. I had sleepless nights!

However, I did witness some small "miracles." Once, one of my brothers brought a partially born chicken, still in its shell. He carried it to my mother. My mother placed a bowl over the egg. She tapped on the bowl—tap, tap, tap—for a long time. Then she raised the bowl, and voila: there you are! The chicken broke loose from its shell, got up, steadied itself, and was able to walk again! At the age of seven, I had witnessed my first miracle!

2.

History of Buxton–Friendship Village Life

For all of us to understand where we are, and how we got here, it's clear we need to understand our history. And that must include the contribution of Africans and their descendants to the story of Britain and the world.
—BEN LONGDEN AND MARTIN BELAM, *THE GUARDIAN*

Buxton–Friendship Village

Buxton-Friendship people are renowned for their determination and grit. That means I came from a long line of strong men and women. These Africans pooled their savings and bought a 500-acre plantation, New Orange Nassau from the owner James Archibald Holmes, for $50,000. They named the village Buxton in honor of abolitionist Thomas Fawell Buxton.[10] Other villages were bought after Buxton. For exam-

---

10. "Purchase of Buxton," Buxton Guyana, http://www.buxtonguyana.net/index_files/Page633.htm.

ple, in November 1839, 83 former African slaves bought the
Victoria Village, also located on the East Coast of Demerara.[11]

After the abolition of slavery on August 1, 1834, my descendants had to purchase, organize, and rebuild their cities. They rebuilt their own places of worship, and they built
schools, colleges, medical clinics, drug stores, and manufacturing industries to buy and sell goods and services within
their communities. The Buxton-Friendship Village is located on the East Coast of Demerara. It lies within Guyana's
Demerara–Mahaica Region 4, approximately 12 miles east
of the capital city of Georgetown. Buxton is on the western
side and Friendship on the eastern portion. According to a
2002 National Census Report, a total of 5,900 persons resided in Buxton and Friendship (3,490 in Buxton and 2,410 in
Friendship).[12]

These were extraordinary feats in light of the fact that
these Africans were former slaves who did not earn much.
They had been enslaved in British Guiana for centuries by
the Dutch and British colonizers. After slavery ended on
August 1, 1834, a system of "apprenticeship" was instituted,
and the freed African slaves were forced to work 40 hours a
week, without pay, on the plantations for four more years. The
Africans earned a pittance for work done in addition to the
40 hours per week. On the other hand, the White slave owners and plantation owners were compensated for the loss of

11. Aubrey Norton, "Pillars of Afro-Guyanese Development," Buxton Guyana,
http://www.buxtonguyana.net/index_files/Page633.htm.
12. "Buxton-Friendship – 170th Anniversary," Guyanese Online, https://
guyaneseonline.files.wordpress.com/2010/03/buxton-friendship-170th-anni-
versary.pdf.

their property by the British crown and government. So it was amazing that the Africans were forced to continue to work on the same plantations where they were enslaved. These funds were used to compensate the slave owners for loss of their human property; yet, the freed slaves were able to save money to buy their own villages.

Further exploitation of the freed slave occurred between 1835 and 1838, when the British marginalized the Africans by inviting European workers to increase the population of White European workers in British Guiana. So, in 1835, small groups of English and German farmers arrived. Then, in 1836, 44 Irish and 47 English and 43 Scottish laborers immigrated to Guyana. However, the population of European laborers could not survive the harsh conditions, working in the tropical climate in Guyana.

Recognizing that the Africans would not continue to work for a pittance now that they were freed, the British put in place orders to undercut access to compensate them. The British imported large numbers of laborers from Asia (Indians and Pakistanis) and Portuguese from Portugal. On May 3, 1835, 553 other Madeirans had arrived in British Guyana as indentured laborers. These laborers were recruited by using public funds saved from unpaid labor of the Africans. On May 5, 1838, a group of 396 laborers arrived in British Guiana from the Indian subcontinent aboard the *Whitby* and the *Hesperus*. The Indian laborers were encouraged to exchange their return passage to India. They were granted a plot of land and a cow after working for five years.

The newcomers were encouraged to maintain their culture and language of origin, unlike the Africans who were stripped of their cultural past, prevented from speaking their native language under pain of death and denied the opportunities to read and write.[13]

In 1853, three ships, the *Glentanner*, the *Lord Elgin*, and the *Samuel Boddington* sailed from Amoy in the Fujian Province of China with 1,549 laborers headed for British Guiana.[14]

Thus, today, Guyana boasts as the country of six nations brought under one flag.[15]

It was under such unbearable circumstances that villages were bought, owned, and administrated by Africans in various parts of Guyana. Under these perverse and oppressive conditions, Buxton and many other villages were born and managed to survive and flourish.

In 1841, the sister village to Buxton, Friendship, was bought. This time, 168 former enslaved slaves bought a 500-acre plantation east of Buxton for $80,000, and the two communities merged to form what is known today as Buxton-Friendship Village. The founders laid out housing plots at the front of the village and designated corresponding farmlands at the back of the village. The villagers established an administrative body, the Buxton-Friendship Village Council, to

---

13. Cristine Khan, "On Anti-Blackness in the Indo-Caribbean Community," Medium, https://medium.com/@cskhan91/on-anti-blackness-in-the-indo-caribbean-community-68bb9f052765.
14. *British West Indies-1838-The Arrival*, DVD, authored by Rohit Jagessar, Kumar Gaurav, and Aarti Bathija (New York: RBC Radio, 2004), https://www.worldcat.org/title/british-west-indies-guiana-1838-the-arrival/oclc/857535684&referer-brief_result.
15. Trey Sue-A-Quan, *Cane Reapers: Chinese Indentured Servants in Guyana* (Vancouver, BC: Cane Press, 2017), https://www.worldcat.org/title/cane-reapers-chinese-indentured-immigrants-in-guyana/oclc/1026409398&referer=brief_results.

manage and maintain infrastructure, build roads, and collect property taxes.[16]

Education and religion were very important to my forefathers. On August 1, 1856, the Methodist Church opened for worship. Then, on November 19, 1871, the Roman Catholic Church was opened for services.

Buxton People Stop Train

People from my village, Friendship and Buxton, are known as "Buxtonians," and there is a famous story of "Buxton People Stopped Train." This famous act has put Buxtonians on the map as one of the most powerful people's groups to ever exist at that time in Guyana's history.[17]

In Guyana and the Caribbean Islands, Buxtonians are proudly renowned for their independence and courage. This reputation was obtained early in the history of British Guiana soon after Buxton Village was established. With the establishment of Buxton as an independent village, the White people who had formerly dictated all aspect of the Africans lives tried every underhanded trick in the book to make them fail. They tried to sabotage the growth of the recently established village by deliberately flooding their farms and tried unsuccessfully to remove them from their homes which were bought through blood, sweat, and tears. The final straw was an unfair taxation of their land by the colonial governing body. Several attempts to dialog with the British governor were ignored.

16. Fitzroy "Rollo" Younge, "Purchase of Friendship," Buxton Guyana, http://buxtonguyana.net/index_files/Page354.htm.
17. Ovid Abrams, "Buxton People Stop Train," Buxton Guyana, http://www.buxtonguyana.net/index_files/Page605.htm.

When news reached the villagers that the governor was going to pass through the village to inspect the recently constructed train lines, they wanted to seize the opportunity to speak with him about the unfair taxation. As the train approach Buxton village, the women of Buxton strode onto the train tracks, literally putting their lives on the "line."

When the train came to a stop, the men and women immobilized the train with chains and locked the wheels. These constrictions prevented the train from moving. The villagers then demanded that the governor address their concerns: exorbitant unfair taxing on their land and to repeal the tax law. Following that bold move on the part of Buxtonians, the governor did repeal the taxes. The story of the brave, fiercely independent, and courageous people of my foreparents' generation lives on![18]

Summer Days in Buxton-Friendship

Summer days in my village could stretch on for what seemed like a lifetime. Villagers looked for opportunities for their children to learn new skills by doing some kind of sports activities, taking piano lessons, typing classes, or summer classes in math and English. None of us children could complain too much because it seemed like the whole village was reading from the same page of this unseen book. Our dad came home one evening and promptly said to my sister and me, "I paid for you all to go and learn shorthand and typing from Mrs. B, in the village." So, for the following year, we walked down to Mrs. B's home and took the fundamentals of

---

18. Ibid.

typing and shorthand. Later, I came to understand the value of learning such skills.

When my sister and I turned 13 and 14 respectively, our aunt insisted that we learn to sew. My mother had an old Singer sewing machine, the kind with the thick belt and big wheels. It sat in a corner of our bedroom for the longest time, and we would throw our used clothes, etc., over it. Once a week, we reluctantly walked to her home, two miles away, to learn to sew. Despite the walk, Aunt Wavney was the kind of aunt that we loved to spend time with. On our arrival, she would have tall glasses of ice-cold fruit juice and some kind of delicious pastries for us. She was gentle, soft spoken, and very talented in many ways. She taught home economics. She knew how to sew, knit, and crochet and was also an excellent cook. She sang in her church choir and was a devoted wife and mother. My sister and I learned how to cut out patterns to make our outfits, and she taught us how to knit and crochet.

These skills came in handy because at the beginning of each school year, when other children got new school uniforms, my parents could not afford to buy us new ones. So my sister and I came up with a plan. Months before school resumed, we would spend hours in our home, carefully loosening the stitches in our old uniform with a razor blade, and turn the garment over (where the sun had not scorched the color). Then we would sew each corner back together and create what looked like new uniforms. To this day, no one except our parents knew what we did throughout our high school years. We graduated to sewing our own clothes and creating our very own styles. We would spend hours designing cool dresses, skirts, tops, and pants. Sewing the crotch area of our pants was the hardest to perfect. We would save up our money, sew our own garments, and dress up like twins. We were admired by many in the village.

Every summer, my sister and I would have to negotiate with our parents to allow us to spend part of our summer breaks with our aunts and cousins in Georgetown, the capital city of Guyana. So, every summer, my sister and I would wash our "good" clothes and iron and fold them neatly. Then, because we could not afford a suitcase, we would use brown paper bags, wrap and tape our clothes into the shape of a bag, and head out to the main public road to hail a taxi to take us to "town."

We'd endure the 30 minutes of loud music blasting from the car speaker and arrive at our Aunt Baby-G's house in Kitty, Georgetown. Other cousins would join us, and for four weeks we would go from one cousin's home to another, enjoying their company, good food, and loads of entertainment. We'd visit the Botanical Gardens and the Audubon Zoo; we also attended circuses and played card games and board games. We had picnics at the beaches and enjoyed the company of our cousins, mostly from my dad's side of the family. Soon it would be time to say our goodbyes and return to the village to resume school.

Wood and Coals

Best friends and the memories that they create in our youth can become some of our most prized possessions. Do you have a childhood friend who still brings a smile to your face recalling the times you had? My best friend was a boy named Monty. He lived next door to me, and his mother was one of my teachers. Monty later became a medical doctor, opened his private practice on the same plot of land where he grew up, and became a successful physician.

Our lives were intertwined from the time we started kindergarten. At the beginning of that school year, the teacher separated us. Monty was a year younger than me, and he saw me as his big sister and did not want to attend school without my presence. Monty coined the term "friend-boy and friend-girl." He got his way; we were inseparable. We were both dreamers.

It was around the late 1960s, and most countries in the world were experiencing regime change or gaining independence from the giants and architects of colonialism—England, France, Spain, and the Dutch. There were frequent news reports and rumors of wars, changing of the guard and alliances, as the world changed. We spent hours pretending that we were rulers of every country in the world. We were to memorize the countries, their capitals, and who was the president or prime minister of each country.

Every other Saturday, Monty's mother would take a trip to Georgetown, and we would roam the neighborhoods, playing yard games like hopscotch; one, two, three red light (which is similar to Simon Says); Chinese jump rope (twisted rubber bands); and gam (like the game of marbles except played with seeds from the awara fruit).

On Monty's mother's return, we would sit on his front porch and enjoy the sweet goodies that she brought back from "town." My godfather, Mr. Younge, named us "Wood and Coals." We would spend most of our waking hours together. If we needed to go to the bathroom, we would take turns going while the other waited for the other to get out. We secretly planned elaborate meals to cook on a fire outside. We were both responsible for stealing items to prepare the meal. I remember once we tried to boil rice over the outdoor fire, but we could not get the fire to stay lit. Another time we tried making our own cigarettes, using the coconut husks wrapped in paper. This, too, was indeed a grave disaster!

When it was time to take the National Common Entrance exams, he was so smart that he obtained one of the highest scores and gained entrance to one of the Ivy League schools in Georgetown. He attended high school in Georgetown and I remained in the village. Although our educational trajectory differed, Monty and I would remain in contact for the rest of his life on earth. We celebrated milestones virtually and remained friends.

Monty—Dr. Montague Hope—had a successful kidney transplant in Manchester, England, in 2004. Unfortunately, my friend lost his battle with kidney disease five years later, in 2009. He was a wonderful husband and father to four children. During our family trip to Guyana in 2018, I had the privilege of introducing my daughters to two of his daughters.

3.

When "Education Was King"

The race of people who do not thirst with assiduity for Education is doomed. You and your children must make the sacrifice. If you don't then the great dreams of the people who brought and established these villages will be undeservedly squandered.[19]
—THE LEGENDARY SIMEON JOSEPHUS "PROPHET" WILLS AT THE DEDICATION OF THE BUXTON MONUMENT IN HONOR OF THE CENTENARY ANNIVERSARY OF EMANCIPATION, 1ST AUGUST, 1938

High School Days

During the early 1960s, Buxton boasted having more educational facilities in one area than other villages on the East Coast of Demerara. There were three secondary schools: Buxton Government Secondary School, County High School,

19. "The Premier Village," Buxton-Friendship, http://www.buxtonguyana.net/index.htm.

and Smith's College. There were four primary schools:
St. Augustine's Anglican School/Friendship Government
School, Friendship Methodist (Wesleyan) School, Arundel
Congregational (Missionary) School, and St. Anthony's
Roman Catholic School. Buxton Village also had its first trade
school or handicraft center to encourage boys and young
men who were interested in learning carpentry, plumbing,
and other technical skills. Students were later transferred to
the Kingston Handicraft Center in Georgetown for further
training.[20]

Buxton High School

In 1973, after graduating from the St. Augustine's Anglican
School/Friendship Government School, I attended the Buxton
Government Secondary School, located on the street where I
lived, Friendship Road, west of the Atlantic Ocean. Students
and teachers came from as far as Plaisance, Beterverwagting,
Enmore, Vigilance, Victoria Village, and others to attend
school in my Buxton-Friendship Village. Remains of the orig-
inal building and its renovations are there today.[21]

Students from out of town would arrive by train, bus, or car
every morning, Monday to Friday, and leave every afternoon.
We locals were happy that we did not have to catch transportation and could walk home. I loved the nineteenth-century
architectural design of the Buxton High School building. It
was a three-storied edifice, made from Greenheart wood,
painted white.[22] It held magnificent, ornate curved window

20. "Buxton-Friendship – 170th Anniversary," guyaneseonline.net.
21. "Purchase of Buxton," buxtonguyana.net.
22. "Architecture," Guyanese Achievers, http://www.guyaneseachievers.com/
architecture/.

and latticed "Demerara shutters" all around the building. These shutters allowed a breeze to enter the open classrooms. The building had a steep pitched gable roof with decorative wooden moldings and louvre shutters and jalousies (windows with slatted louvres).

Whenever it rained, some students were assigned to close the windows while others closed them before we left in the afternoons after school ended. When we arrived in the morning, the windows would already have been opened by the custodians. Guyana is a tropical country. Throughout the year, temperatures fluctuated from 70 degrees in the morning to a high of 90 degrees at midday. The architectural design of the structure reflected the environment, the culture, and the technological and historical context in which we lived.

The ground floor held one of my favorite places to be, the Buxton-Friendship Village Library, and on the opposite side were the biology and physics labs as well as a chemistry department. Students entered the building from either of two sets of wooden stairs which merged into a balcony. Then we went up a longer flight of stairs that held another balcony. There was a wide double door which opened into the main floor. Classes were held there, in open classrooms. There was a narrow path to let one head straight and then turn, only left to enter the door that led to another flight of stairs or across the hallway to more classrooms. Upstairs, the classrooms were enclosed; that was where senior level courses were taught. In the music room, located next to the classrooms, there was an array of drums, steelpan drums, and musical accoutrements.

The distance from the main public road (East Coast Demerara Road), heading east and back west, was a manageable walk for students and teachers. At 7:30 a.m., during the week, the rhythmic sound of feet traversed the brick and asphalt road, waking every animal around and sending them scurrying for safety under the shrubs along the roadside.

Everyone was trying to get to school by 8:00 a.m. Then the streets quieted until it was 3:30 p.m., and the sounds came again, from east to west, as students and teachers headed out of the village once more. Sometimes we remained after school to practice steelpan music or to play volleyball and ping-pong. However, I often headed to the library to sit and read or do my homework.

Bladen Hall Multilateral Secondary School

Change throws some kids off. Did you ever have to change schools? In the beginning of my high school term in 1973, we were notified that the government was building a state-of-the-art school, the Bladen Hall Multilateral Secondary School, located in Bladen Hall on the East Coast of Demerara. It was about one mile away from my home in Friendship. This secondary school design of educational facilities was the brainchild of then president of Guyana, L.F.S. Burnham. The goal of this new institution was to provide students with a comprehensive high school education. The program emphasized practical application, "in pursuit of perfection." The campus housed teachers in separate two-story brick buildings, surrounded by beautiful, manicured lawns, and a sports complex.

I was upset about the new location. Not only could we not afford to buy a bicycle, but this meant no more lunches at home. Thus, when school reopened in September 1975, my sister and I had to walk from Friendship, past the Brusche Dam, then Traspey Village to finally get to school every day.

We would prepare our lunch the night before and carry it in our lunch pack, along with our backpack, to school and back every day.

Eventually, I got used to walking to and from school. Unlike the crowded classrooms at the Buxton High School, Bladen Hall High was a massive three-storied structure, L-shaped and made from concrete. There were enclosed stairways at the opposite ends of the building and at the center of the structure. Every classroom looked the same to me. Unlike Buxton High, where each teacher came to teach us in our classrooms, we had to go find our next classrooms every 35 to 45 minutes. And, to make matters worse, each room was painted the same drab grayish blue and yellow, and some areas sported light pink shades. I would rush out to get to the next class before I realized that I had headed in the wrong direction and had to turn around to try and run to make it to class on time. I got lost several times before I figured out how to compartmentalize the building's design in my mind's eye.

There were some good things about the school. The ground floor held classrooms for arts and crafts, including pottery making, weaving, etc. Students who were interested in learning about farming, woodworking, agriculture, engineering, and home economics got to explore those areas of study. Some of us got to play ping-pong, softball, badminton, gymnastics, hockey, soccer, and track and field and cricket. The fields were wide open, and sometimes at lunch time, we sat outside and enjoyed the cool breeze before the bell rang for us to return to our classrooms.

I recall the first time my school's ping-pong team won the local area tournament and had to travel to Georgetown to compete against the Ivy League schools—St. Rose's High, Bishop

High, and Queen's College along with Central High and other area schools. On arrival, I felt intimidated by the sheer number of students dressed in like-colored sports uniforms and matching tennis shoes. We had just managed to put together whatever shorts and t-shirts we could find. I felt out of place.

They would gather in groups to practice as I watched from afar. I was mesmerized by the dexterity and skill of the ping-pong players. Right then, I knew we did not belong there. For the first time in my life, I felt inadequate and unworthy.

The tournament was scheduled for Friday night and the following day, Saturday. Our team did not make it to Saturday. We lost in the first round, then got a chance to compete again and lost again.

We did compete in other areas, such as badminton, gymnastics, and in track and field and soccer. We won some and lost some. Years later, my youngest sister, Nola, would gain the second highest score on the Common Entrance Exam in our village and receive a scholarship to attend the Central High School in Georgetown. In 2019, Central High merged with St. Mary's High and was renamed New Central High School.

I am proud to say that I was part of the first graduating class of Bladen Hall Secondary School, in 1977. Several of my classmates have gone on to have successful careers. Eusi Kwayana, in the compilation of the book *Buxton-Friendship in Print and Memory*, has recorded the fact that Buxtonians have individually and collectively made a difference in the fields of education, business, medicine, public service, sports, music, and entertainment in Guyana and abroad.[23]

---

23. Rennie Parris, "The Emancipation Covenant," Buxton Guyana, http://buxtonguyana.net/index_files/Page552.htm.

As for me, after graduating from secondary school in 1977, my godmother called me over to her home and sat me down. She wanted to know my plans for the future. There are many of us who are ready to explain our plans to conquer the world. I was not one of those people. I told her I was not sure. She encouraged me to apply to be a student teacher and then, if I liked it, I could apply to go on to train as a teacher.

I applied and received an invitation in the mail for an interview. I hurriedly ran over to show her the letter. She appeared very excited and, unbeknownst to me, had recruited her daughter, who was part of the Ministry of Education Department at that time, to invite me to an interview in Georgetown. I had never been interviewed by anyone in my life. I did not know what to wear or how to dress for the occasion. I eventually chose a favorite dress that I had sewn with my sister. The only thing missing to complete my attire was a handbag. My mom overheard me complaining that I had no handbag to match my outfit, so she borrowed a family friend's handbag for me to use for the interview.

I remember arriving early for the interview and trying to remember what I had written in my application about myself. When I was called into the room, I was so nervous, I could not speak clearly, and I could not even remember what the title of the position was to which I had applied. It was downright embarrassing.

However, I got my first assignment as a pupil teacher for a grade school in the village of Victoria (on the East Coast of Demerara) under the direction of Mrs. Ainsworth. I learned how to teach on the job, and she challenged me to learn and teach ballet to first- and second-grade students. In order to learn the basic steps in ballet, I looked at magazines and read about the basic ballet positions.

In ballet, there are five basic positions of the feet and three dance movements that beginning students must learn. Position 1: Stand with heels together and toes facing equally out to either side (heels touch). Position 2: Stand in first position (Position 1) with feet about hip distance apart. Position 3: This is rarely done. Start in first then move the heel of your feet to the middle, to the middle of the other. Legs remain straight. Position 4: Place one foot in front of the other (one full foot distance apart). Legs and feet are equally turned out away from the center of the body. The final, Position 5, is the most difficult one. Stand with your feet close together, one in front of the other and turned away from the body. While in this position, one has to maintain a straight leg and be prepared to jump and land perfectly.

Now these are the dance movements: Plie (plee-ay): to bend, releve (ruh-leh-vay): to rise, and sante (soh-tay): to jump.[24]

I taught the students the basic positions and movements and paired them with music to dance to. When I met Mrs. Ainsworth's daughter, Holly, we became best friends. She was also one of my greatest cheerleaders. This was by no means an easy task for an 18-year-old rookie, like me. I think the kids had more fun than I did most of the time!

Years later, when I immigrated to the United States, watching the ice skating Olympians display those moves seamlessly

24. See https://ballethub.com/.

on ice was a marvel to behold, for I know how difficult that has to be under such pressure.

After nine months at Victoria, I applied to several of the Guyana government sectors and accepted a job at the Ministry of Finance Department in Georgetown. I worked there for three years as an accounts clerk 1.

Someone said, "You might be happier someplace else, but remember you still have to take you, with you."

I became restless and was aware that I was in a dead-end job. Every day, hundreds of us arrived at work and sat at individual desks. We logged enormous binders, stacked alphabetically from giant metal bookshelves, hauled them to our desks, and kept track of persons, organizations, and companies that were delinquent in paying taxes and other financial obligations. We were responsible for contacting them and encouraging them to pay up . . . or else. During our lunch breaks, we played dominoes and card games. I made a few friends, and that helped, but I wondered how I could ever get ahead in such an environment. I needed to find a way to escape the drudgery.

Education always seems like the solution when you find yourself wondering how you are going to move forward and achieve more. So I enrolled in the Critchlow Labor College, located on Wolford Avenue, Thomas Lands, Georgetown. I attended classes at nights before heading home late in the evening. I then turned around and headed back to work the next day. Monday to Friday, I would travel by public transportation from Friendship Village to Main and Urquhart Street in Georgetown for work, and after finishing work, I would take the bus to attend college. Most nights I slept on the bus or in the taxi on my way home. I graduated with a diploma in industrial sciences and an understanding of what it takes to become an entrepreneur. Armed with this new knowledge, I felt proud of my accomplishment. So, while in conversation with a friend, he encouraged me to seek opportunities elsewhere.

4.

Going to America

We all have dreams. In order to make dreams come into reality, it takes an awful lot of determination, dedication, self-discipline, and effort.
—JESSE OWENS, WORLD RECORD-SETTING OLYMPIC ATHLETE

My Parents' Journey

A good life cannot be measured by the number of candles on a cake, but by the people whose lives you touched and who have touched yours. My philosophy is that our lives pivot on the dreams we have seen come true and the ones we are still working on. When we remember the joyful times, when life was easy, and the challenging times when faith saw us through, we know we have done our utmost best.

I can still remember the last time I saw and held my mom. In 1983, at the young age of 48 years, she had a stroke. She had aged tremendously. I was shaken to my core when she tried to stand up to greet me, but she needed to be careful. Once she did, I could see the error, the drag in her right leg. The way she held up her right arm close to her side sealed the deal for me.

I shed tears and she said, "Don't worry, Caryl, I'm doing better."

I realized that Mom worked so hard. She made our home beautiful. Mom's wedding cakes were lovely and made her famous in our village. We never got a chance to celebrate her.

I wondered how it must have felt for my mom, an active leader in her church, a hardworking young woman, to wake up that morning, unable to feel or touch on the right side of her body, down to her feet. Her body feeling like it was on fire, then parts of her body refusing to function as usual. I'll never know how frustrating that must have felt for her. I never asked. It was not the right time. Or was it?

She and my father had looked forward to immigrating to the United States with my younger sister, Nola. My older sister, Ingrid, had just given birth to a baby boy. My parents seemed happy back then. But overshadowing my parents' excitement was the political situation in Guyana. Life had become almost unbearable for them. My father had just lost his job, yet again. For over 45 years he had given his all, working in the sugar cane fields, sweat around his waist, perspiration dripping down his face. He had hauled, then punted sugar cane down the river. He worked for private and government projects as a carpenter, painter, builder of bridges, and as a foreman for a construction site. His stellar resume could not prevent him from getting laid off. It was the early 1980s and things had gone south for the country. The leaders in the country of Guyana were trying a new way of political system: socialism.

In 1972, the Guyana government introduced free education, from kindergarten to the university level. This was hurriedly put together after the then president L.F.S. Burnham returned from one of his many trips to the Union of Soviet Socialist Republics (the USSR). No thought was given to assess whether the Guyana economy could bear the cost and strain to fund another program.

With this program in full swing, the National Service program was introduced, whereby all graduates from the major university, the University of Guyana, had to sign a contract to serve the country for three years in any of the eight military or paramilitary forces or organizations. This system of "dual control" did not bode well with the Guyanese citizenry. Soon, children were taken out of school without parental permission to participate in "Mass Games" (similar to the Olympics performances during the opening ceremony) to perform for the president and his Soviet friends on their visit to Guyana.

In 1977, a slogan was introduced. It said, "The Small Man Will Become a Real Man!" Vast amounts of money were invested in housing programs, and in two years the number of private homeowners rose remarkably. This resulted in an increased need for more public transportation. New busses were imported from India. This put many private car and cab drivers out of work.

In the early 1980s, another slogan came out. It said, "Guyanese Must Be Self-Sufficient!" All imported food and nonessential commodities, car parts, gasoline, etc., were banned from being imported. Almost overnight, the price of a barrel of cooking oil skyrocketed from $25 to $95 a barrel. Basic food items became scarce and people had to line up to buy groceries. Because most people had a vegetable garden in their backyard, vegetables were still available to purchase.

Every night on the news, Guyanese were being encouraged
to produce their own local flour to make bread. They were
to be self-reliant. Everywhere there were signs posted along
the road that encouraged people to produce or perish! The
government took possession of private stores. After a short
time, the stores were closed. The cost of living was very high.

For the first time in my life, I woke up to find my dad at
home on Monday, then Tuesday, and finally every day of the
week. He and my mom spoke in undertones, and sometimes
when we were around, they would stop speaking. After he got
laid off, friends in the village were giving him unsolicited advice about how to get his job back. He knew that would be
impossible. My father was very practical. He said, "I'm gonna
find work, don't bother."

He continued to look for work. In those days, Dad became a softer, gentler version of himself. Meanwhile, he spent
quality time with my youngest sister, Nola. Dad exercised
by running and walking with her alongside the seawall. She
was at an age when she really needed her dad. He helped her
with her studies by prepping her for a major exam that all
Guyanese sixth graders took to matriculate to a number of Ivy
League secondary schools in Georgetown. Nola received the
second highest score in the village for the Common Entrance
Examination the year she took the exam.

Then, early one morning, I awoke to the familiar sounds
of activities in the dining room. I opened my eyes, and saw a
man dressed in a navy-blue uniform. At first, I thought I was
still dreaming. After a while, I recognized my dad. His face
was clean shaven. He was dressed in complete regalia of that
of a guard, shiny shoes and all. He left home shortly after, and
later when I asked my mother where he had gone, she said,

"Your dad has to find work. The only work is guard work these days." So my dad faithfully went back to doing what he loved best, working! My dad worked as a guard until he, my mother, and youngest sister received permission to immigrate to the United States of America on April 15, 1983. He had given his absolute best; however, he had to begin anew!

"That may be true, but I think God has a plan. Maybe if more people like you and I get with God's agenda, then America might experience the greatest racial reconciliation in our churches. Then could you imagine what would happen when that spills out from the church into society?"

—June Wood Agamah

5.

Life in Barbados

No one is exempted from the zagged edge of living in this world. How should we look forward to heaven when everything on earth is hunky-dory?

—ANONYMOUS

My journey to Barbados was by no means well planned. I had worked at the Ministry of Finance at 49 Main and Urquhart Street in Georgetown for three years as an account clerk 1. I was in my early 20s, and I was awaiting my "green card" (the permanent resident card that allowed me to live and work permanently in the United States).[25] My Aunt Olga Schultz, a Guyanese-American citizen at that time (in the 1980s), had applied for her brother (my father, Howell) and his minor children to join her and her family, as permanent residents, to live the United States.

---

25. US Citizenship and Immigration Services, "Bringing Siblings to Live in the United States as Permanent Residents," USCIS, https://www.uscis.gov/family/family-of-us-citizens/bringing-siblings-to-live-in-the-united-states-as-permanent-residents.

It was the early 1980s. The Jackson Five, an American rhythm and blues/pop music group, a worldwide sensation, was on the verge of splitting and Michael Jackson's solo, "Thriller" was breaking all kinds of records. Michael Jackson became one of the best-known celebrities on the planet![26]

At that time, in the early 1980s, most Caribbean countries were encouraging travel between Guyana and other CARICOM countries. Obtaining a visitor's visa to any of the 15 countries was easy. These countries—Grenada, Jamaica, Barbados, Dominica, Guyana, Antigua and Barbuda, Saint Lucia, Belize, Haiti, Surinam, Trinidad and Tobago, Saint Vincent and the Grenadines, Saint Kitts and Nevis, and the Bahamas—were classified as developing countries. Although small in size and diverse in geography and language, they covered an area of 177,000 square miles. Members operate as a regional single market and have advantage in handling regional trade disputes. According to the Treaty of Chaguaramas of the Caribbean Community in 1973, which has its headquarters in Georgetown, members shall be open to promoting economic integration and corporation among its members, thus removing barriers to trade, goods, and services among the nations.

Barbados is one of the islands that is part of the Lesser Antilles, and the official language is English. It is one of the more populous Caribbean islands. Like Guyana, Barbados

---

26. *Encyclopedia of African American Pop Culture [4 volumes]*, ed. Jessie Carney Smith, (Santa Barbara, CA: ABC-CLIO, 2010), 746, https:// books.google.com/books?id=10rEGSIItjgC&pg=PA746&lpg=PA746&d-q=The+Jackson+Five+beginning+popularity&source=bl&ots=AU7Pbk-TYOV&sig=ACfU3U2Kag4fPb304pSvZDaXIkW5Ae7n-w&hl=en&sa=X-&ved=2ahUKEwjB9Jn_6azqAhWaZs0KHZOJDN0Q6AEwEXoE-CA0QAQ#v=onepage&q=The%20Jackson%20Five%20beginning%20popularity&f=false.

gained independence from Britain in 1966. However, Guyana
became a republic four years after, in 1970. But Barbados has
remained under the Queen Elizabeth monarchy.[27]

I chose to immigrate to Barbados at the time because a
close Guyanese acquaintance who resided there invited me to
explore opportunities for work. I considered the possibility of
furthering my education by obtaining a degree in education. I
thought I could maybe become a teacher. Or what about those
other jobs that my friend had convinced me abounded in that
country? In fact, after further investigation, I discovered that
many of the career opportunities were in the tourism industry.

Another phase would be that of applying for a work per-
mit. For a foreign-born applicant, this process is difficult.
Barbados is a small island with a high percentage of skilled
laborers. Thus, the competition for the best jobs is very high. I
had made the decision to follow my instincts, to take the risk
and look for opportunities outside of Guyana. So Barbados
was my first stop.[28]

It was the summer of 1982, and as the aircraft descended
its course to land at the Barbados Grantley Adams Airport,[29]
the sound of excitement could be captured in the voices of
passengers. One could hear the laughter from adults on board
the flight and the chattering of small children over the hum
of the British Airways Flight as they peered through the windows at the circular motion giving us the view of tiny dots of

27. "Member States of the Caribbean Community," Wikipedia, https://en.wiki-
pedia.org/wiki/Member_states_of_the_Caribbean_Community.
28. A Google search of "Careers in Barbados" generated approximately 206
million results.
29. "Grantley Adams International Airport," Wikipedia, https://en.wikipedia.
org/wiki/Grantley_Adams_International_Airport.

white, red, and green homes set amid the green, lush fields. I could not determine different kinds of foliage from where I sat but saw shades of greens and browns interspersed by neatly mowed grass on the golf courses. All these seemed to be held at bay by the bowl-shaped blue and white water of the Atlantic Ocean. The dark blue sky descended into blueish-gray as the skyline merged with the light-blue ocean. As the tail of the aircraft became level with the tarred airstrip, everyone clapped in unison! We could no longer see the ocean. We had landed safely in Barbados.

Traveling By Bus, Bajan Style

Traveling on the city bus in Barbados was very interesting. People tended to extend politeness to each other almost effortlessly. If someone got on the bus with several parcels and/ or with children, the closest sitting person got up to allow that person to sit comfortably. Men and boys rose up immediately when they saw that elderly men and women entered the bus. On closer investigation of the previous observation, I learned that Barbadians prided themselves on the image that winning friends and influencing people was key to success in the tourist industry on the bus everywhere during my stay in Barbados.

The island's beaches provide its people with opportunities for relaxation. The beaches attract tourists as well as islanders.[30] The traffic always seemed to be gravitating toward the beach areas. Most important political and civil discourse were held in the vicinity of the beaches. People from all over the

---

30. Erica Walsh, "Best Barbados Beaches," Travel Channel, https://www. travelchannel.com/interests/beaches/articles/best-barbados-beaches.

world, like me at that time, would congregate, and after much rallying the crowd dissipated just like it had congregated. Sometimes, a few people remained by the water in groups and held private picnics. Some would go diving, sailing, or swimming. As evening drew near, people returned to their homes, leaving in its wake the steady wish-washing sound of the water. The beach appeared desolate and black, and it extended for miles as the lights from the streetlights cast reflections on the now dark-blue water.

My Visit to Cultural Markers

Family vacations, traveling, and history all have so much in common. We gain our love for different places through the travel to those places. For me, I think my love for national parks began in Barbados. Parks elicit a degree of sacredness in my spirit. They have so much for one to observe, listen to, and do. Often these green and colorful breathtaking landscapes and beautiful expanses are located in the center of incredibly busy cities. I often go to parks to discover new things and to center myself. As I wander around, I often sense that the God of the universe illuminates the relational nature of Himself. It is a place to love and relax the mind.

Botanical gardens are often located within national parks. This is where my mind sees patterns of life in the lush acres of shrubs, trees, flowers, and wildlife. I could spend hours oohing and aahing over the intricate designs in flowers and shrubs. The pastures of sweet ferns and juniper go on and on in the summer, but how sad, they too will change with the seasons, unlike the cultural markers, which remain with their innocent and tranquil designs intact throughout the year. So it was that simple lesson that inspired me. Armed with the currency of time on my hand, I became an avid tourist.

Barbados is known as Little England. The country is synonymous with England in that they are both islands.[31] Barbados's political history must have had something to do with the nickname, in that it was a British colony. Barbados has claimed the name and has used it to influence her prospects in the development of her most dependable resource, tourism. Because of the country's geographic location, Barbados enjoys tropical weather throughout the year. It is an ideal tourist destination due to its natural beauty.

Like most islands, Barbados is surrounded by beautiful beaches.[32] The Atlantic Ocean enfolds the 660 square miles of anticlines. Thus, the city of Bridgetown, which lies in the northern part of the country, appears to be overflowing into the Atlantic Ocean. There are architectural remains of castles dotting the town and rural areas.

One castle that I loved to visit was the Sam Lord's Castle. The castle sprawled at the southern tip of the island and was very ancient. There was a story that Sam Lord was a great king who lived in the castle. He was a great sailor. He had men working with him at sea. On the edge of the castle, there was a huge lamp. Sailors would stop at the castle and Sam Lord's sailors would trick the sailors by enticing them to stay on the island. During the night, he would kill the visitors and steal their treasures.

---

31. Hoyos, "Little England," *Planet Barbados* (blog).
32. Walsh, "Barbados Beaches," travelchannel.com.

During my visit to the castle in 1983, there were displays in the hotel. There were exhibits of Sam Lord's weapons, knives, and swords along with displays of hooks, boats, nets, and a number of tools used by him and his men. Maybe because of the intrigue, the castle served as one of the best tourist attractions in the 1980s. There were also displays of beautiful cutlery, paintings, monuments, furniture, and accessories worn by the women of the castle.[33] Unfortunately, in 2010, a fire destroyed this castle. In 2020, a new hotel replaced the old historic one.[34] I am forever grateful that I was able to visit the Sam Lord's Castle in the 1980s. Most of the above were destroyed in the fire. What a pity that the island of Barbados lost one of its national treasures forever.

Then there are the remains of the Central Park Castle, situated in what is now considered a public park. This castle overlooked the entire island of Barbados.[35] As I looked at the site during one of my visits, it reminded me of the pre-medieval era in the city of Rome. I stood on the remains of a stairway and what I saw surprised me. The view of the city of Bridgetown below looked magnificent! The houses appeared like dwarfs and the traffic seemed to be winding in and out of the mountain peaks. The lush green of the grassland changed its color and the mountains became valleys and the valleys became fields of potato plants or sugar cane plants. The river

33. Wikipedia, "Samuel Hall Lord," https://en.wikipedia.org/wiki/Samuel_Hall_Lord.
34. "Sam Lord's Castle," Barbados, https://barbados.org/samlords.htm#.XxDbjmhKg2w.
35. A Google search for "Central Park Castle" generated more than 78 million results.

seemed almost dark blue as the crooked coconut trees and palm trees cast their shadows over the water. As I looked further, the constant bubbling up and down of a head or two along with the many-colored sailboats and surf boats appeared in the water. People seemed to be everywhere along the beach. Occasionally, the wind would uproot a tent and as the occupants hurried to retrieve it, I felt myself caught up with the anxiety of preventing the tent's departure to freedom.

I stood there much longer than I had planned, and I heard the tantalizing crescendo of Bob Marley's voice. Groups of people had crowded around the jukebox (this was once replaced by a boom box back then) and as others passed by, they danced for a while and then moved on. Busloads of people emerged, and the crowd had engulfed them once again as more people came and went, adding colors of blues and yellows mixed with pinks, reds, and purples, which only added to the number of people and colors.

Years later, I was reminded of Central Park in Barbados when I visited New York Central Park with our middle daughter, Aseye, a graduate student at Columbia University in New York. We took a stroll from her dorm room and we walked through endless layers of ravine. I remembered my time in Barbados and was shaken by the many sites, iconic structures, and historical features that surrounded us. The vibrant colors of orange and yellows against the backdrop of the puffy white then blueish sky, all surrounded by reservoirs, ponds, and lakes, was a photographer's paradise. During our self-guided tour, we read about the fact that this park has been fodder for the likes of movie producers of popular American films like *Breakfast at Tiffany's, When Harry Met*

Sally, Enchanted and *The Avengers!*[36] This all began to make sense once we discovered how much money was spent each year to develop and continue to maintain such ginormous spaces of beauty. After all, there is purpose in the preservation of these endless acreages (spanning 3.5 square miles, 843 acres, seven bodies of water, 1,400 species of flora, 58 miles of hiking trails, 29 sculptures, etc.). The sheer beauty and size is something to behold and it seared into my mind that the thing we share across continents is the incredible creation God has placed before us to see Him within.

36. "Strolling Central Park, an Endless Walk," Marmara NYC, https://park.marmaranyc.com/strolling-central-park-endless-walk/.

"That may be true, but I think God has a plan. Maybe if more people like you and I get with God's agenda, then America might experience the greatest racial reconciliation in our churches. Then could you imagine what would happen when that spills out from the church into society?"

—June Wood Agamah

6.

My Journey to America

*Those who say it can't be done are usually
interrupted by others doing it.*
—JAMES BALDWIN ON SUCCESS

Heeding the Call

More often than not, we make choices with expectations
that don't work out the way we planned. Ever make plans and
have them just fall apart?

A month after my arrival in Barbados, I could not find
work, so a friend introduced me to a couple who had three
beautiful, young daughters. They were busy people. He was
a successful lawyer and she a businesswoman. They invited
me to stay at their lovely home in an upscale neighborhood
in Bridgetown, Barbados. I lived in the basement in a large
one-bedroom furnished apartment. I had my own space,
bathroom, and a full kitchen area. I was very content. I served
the family with gusto! They often held parties and gatherings
upstairs and in their backyard area. I learned how to prepare

"Bajan" cuisine and tempered that with some of my favorite Guyanese dishes.

Most of the family loved my cooking, but one of the girls did not like to eat. I sometimes convinced her to come sit in my lap, like my mom did when I was little, and she would take a few bites. In order to get her to eat, I told her stories about my mother's cooking in Guyana. As the storytelling progressed, the rest of the family would draw near to listen. A story about my mother would be like this:

"My mother, Walterine, was one of the best pastry makers and cake maker/decorators in Buxton-Friendship Village. Everyone knew her as the best maker of black pudding (a delicacy similar to tureso sausage),[37] black cake (a traditional Guyanese/West Indian cake made from a variety of dried fruits soaked for a month in Guyana Rum), and sponge cake (white cake). Every day my mom sold cheese rolls, pine tarts, and beef patties to workers at the local garment factory during lunchtime. My youngest sister at the time would assist her before returning to school.

"On Saturday afternoons, my neighbors and people in the village were treated to some of my mother's famous delicacies. She prepared a basket filled with black pudding in a bowl. This sat next to a container of souse (a combination of meat, cucumbers, vinegar, salt, and peppers).[38] She walked the streets to sell her creations to the delight of her patrons. She returned

---

37. "Guyanese Black Pudding," Fandom, https://recipes.fandom.com/wiki/Guyanese_Black_Pudding.
38. Real Nice Guyana, "Chicken Foot Souse," YouTube video, 10:09, July 9, 2017, https://www.youtube.com/watch?v=SIReA1PNKwM.

home, smiling from ear to ear, with an empty basket and a pocket full of money.

"She catered for weddings, parties, and baby and wedding showers. I remember staring intently as my mom deftly created hundreds of beautifully formed roses made out of icing, set against the green leaves, to create wonderful designs of towering two-, three-, or four-tiered cakes. The last phase would be the placing of the bride and groom on top. I often got the honor of doing so. People in the village would talk about my mom's wedding cakes for months after a wedding party was over and, to this day, whenever I go for walks in the village, I am known as 'Caryl, one of Walterine's daughters.'

"My mother knew the art of shared burden of lending long before the cooperative system was coined. She managed to encourage 10 women to contribute $50 every week to her 'box hand' program. At the end of the month, one woman received the total amount to use however she needed. They took turns doing this and were able to become self-reliant women in those days when access to bank loans was limited. My sister Ingrid and I benefited the most. Since my mother was the most popular caterer and wedding cake maker, most brides wanted us to be the flower girls in their weddings. So my mom used some of her savings to buy beautiful clothes and shoes for us to attend the weddings and bought new furniture and curtains for our home.

"My mom taught us girls how to clean, cook, bake, and be hospitable. We had weekly 'inside' assignments. Mine was to mix, knead, plait, and bake homemade bread every Saturday. The final products were masterpieces from my perspective. My mother and I would carefully wrap each light-brown loaf in wax paper and place them in a woven basket that hung from a nail protruding from the rafter in the middle of the kitchen. The smell of fresh bread would envelop the kitchen for a few days and then fade into the other scents of freshly baked pine tarts, cheese rolls, and meat pies.

"During those days, everyone loved to pay our family a visit. My mom always had mouthwatering pastries, breads, coconut buns, pine tarts, beef and chicken patties, and other snacks to offer her visitors. She exuded a kind, warm, and gentle spirit and, to this day, I attribute some of my personal habits and bent to that of her genealogy.

"My fondest memories of my mother were laying my head on her chest, listening to her heartbeat. Whenever I was ill and could not eat, she would patiently feed me my meals, and every morsel tasted like candy because it came from the hand of one who loved me the most!

"My mother was a 'healer' by nature. She knew no one as a stranger. She knew about herbs, folk medicines, and solutions for healing and comfort. I remember watching people come to our home, bent over in pain. My mom would tend to them, and I would watch in amazement as they left my home, walking upright with smiles on their faces. My mom grew herbs around our yard. I still recall her gentle voice, saying, 'Caryl, go pick some lemon grass, daisy, tea-zum, calabash leaf, or sweet broom tea to boil for the tea.' I became knowledgeable about each herbal tea. I would scamper down the back stairs, pluck and gather a sample in my hand, and return to the kitchen. She would wash the herbs under running water and let them boil in a pot. Then, as we sat around the dining room table, she strained freshly brewed tea into our cups, adding milk and sugar. It was the best tea-drinking experience ever!"

By the time I finished telling them stories about my mother, they had all eaten every morsel off their plates.

* * *

I spent most of the day cleaning, washing, and cooking until the children returned from school and their parents arrived from work. Sometimes, I would receive visits from my Guyanese friends during the day, but the majority of my time was spent taking care of the family. Until, one day, I received an unexpected visit from my friend Norris Henry. He is from Guyana also. Norris is the kind of friend that everyone needs in their life. He is like the golden retriever . . . very positive about everything and everyone. He could make your worst enemy look like a saint. He would show up, armed with several cassette tapes. For those of you who play music on MP3 and other shiny discs, cassettes were tiny plastic boxes filled with high-quality music.

My relationship with Norris was a loving/uncomfortable one. My life was a lonely life in many respects, so I looked forward to his visits. It was a break in the monotony and provided adult conversation about back home (Guyana). However, instead of popular music of the day, his cassettes were filled with recorded contemporary Christian music and concerts. Sometimes he would show up, beaming from ear to ear. "Caryl, you have to hear this message. It's great!" I would listen to the messages, and although I was not very impressed, I nodded politely. I was unfamiliar with his world but could not help but admire Norris's exuberance. The joy on his face said it all. I just hadn't reached a place yet where my faith felt like those messages were made for me.

The best (and most fun) times for me were when the children came home and we would belt out Michael Jackson songs on the tape recorder or tune into channels that featured him and his brothers. We would watch his videos and try to imitate his dance moves. Then we would buckle up our roller skates and whisk and waltz across the smooth linoleum floor. It was a fun time, indeed!

Then, like everything in my life, change happened suddenly. . . .

I was still taking my evening shower when I received the call. In those days, communication was only by landline phones. The first mobile phone model, the Mobira Senator, came out in 1982 and weighed 9.8 kg. It was 1983, and the Nokia's first "handheld" mobile phone, the Mobies Cityman 900, became available in 1989. It weighed 800g.[39]

The ordinary man did not have ready access to such things as cell phones and computers. So when someone called and it was for you, you needed to pick up the telephone. I heard one of the girls calling me, "Caryl, the phone is for you!" I quickly dried off, covered myself with a towel, and grabbed the phone.

It was my Cousin Eunice on the other end of the line. She was calling from Slidell. It was a little over two months since my parents had arrived in the United States. They had to have settled in nicely in rural Slidell, since they were accustomed to living in the village in Guyana. It was early summer, so they

39. Richard Goodwin, "The History of Mobile Phones from 1973 to 2008: The Cellphones That Made It All Happen," Know Your Mobile Phone, https://www.knowyourmobile.com/phones/the-history-of-mobile-phones-from-1973-to-2008-the-handsets-that-made-it-all-happen-d58/.

would enjoy the weather. *I had not spoken to them in a while,* I thought, *so surely, she just wants to check in.*

She asked, "How are you, Caryl?"

"I am doing quite well, and you?" I replied.

And then she asked, "Are you sitting down?"

I told her I was. I sensed right away that something was not right. So I asked her what was wrong, and she said, "Caryl, we lost Cousin Walterine!"

My mother had died!

I must have screamed, because I heard several footsteps running down the stairs in my direction. I felt numb. The next few days were a nightmare. I had to apply to the US Embassy in Barbados for permission to obtain a family bereavement visa to travel from Barbados to the United States, then I had to make arrangements to book my flight to the United States. I had to contact my siblings and relatives to share the horrible news. My sweet mother had just turned 49 years.

She, my dad, and my sister Nola had received their immigration papers and left Guyana in March 1983 to arrive in America. They had arrived in Slidell, full of hope; they dreamt of working hard to save enough money to apply for the rest of their adult children to join them in the United States of America. Unfortunately, my dad could not find work. My mother needed medicine to continue her care after the initial stroke she had before leaving Guyana for America. It was only two months later, and she was gone!

This became a pivotal moment in my life. For the first time in my life, I was experiencing the greatest loss and I had no anchor. Growing up as a child in Guyana, I knew about God, but I did not know Him and that He cared to know me. Whenever I looked up in the skies, I felt that there was something up there, but whatever it was, was unreachable. On a clear day, I would stand in my backyard, next to the vegetable garden, and spin my little self around while looking up in the sky. When I felt dizzy, I would flop to the ground and let my mind imagine myself in the presence of God. However, when my sister and I took confirmation classes at the small Methodist church in Friendship, dressed in white dresses, white stockings, white gloves, and white hair bows in our hair, I was just going through the motions. This rite of passage was expected of young men and ladies. Our brothers refused to do the same, but my sister and I wanted to do so. Now I wondered, *Is there a God? And can He help me get through this?*

Did God really care about my situation? I wondered. *If He cared, why did He take my mom at such an early age?* Anguished questions kept running through my mind.

I decided that day that I was going to test Him. I was scheduled to go to an interview for my visa to the United States the next morning and I was apprehensive for a number of reasons. First, I had overstayed my time in Barbados, and second, it was a troubling season in the world.

US President Ronald Reagan had just passed the Caribbean Basin Initiative (CBI) on February 24, 1982. The United States was deepening its involvement in the conflict brewing in the Caribbean. There were conflicts within El Salvador and there was fear that it would spill elsewhere. Boatloads of Haitians and Cubans, Mexican narcotics trafficking, and a porous border were concerns for the United States.

President Reagan wanted to crack down on illegal immigration to the United States. The US Navy and Coast Guards were losing the battle. Nicaragua was being defiant, Cuba unrestrained, Grenada was oblivious to the state of affairs in its own country, and it was difficult for the United States to play a role in combating most of these problems. So, in a speech to the Organization of American States (OAS), President Reagan unveiled a plan of action. He promoted political stability and economic development in the region and wanted to crack down on illegal immigration. He encouraged one-way free trade, investment incentives in the private sector, and special help to Puerto Rico and the Virgin Islands. These proposals, he hoped, would stop the "sinking" bowl.[40] In retrospect, these proposals worked to stabilize things; now, 40 years later, the Caribbean nations are more zealous and accepting of their sovereignty.

It was against this background that the evening before going to bed, I prayed, *Lord, whoever you are, please help me to succeed in obtaining a visa from the US Embassy to the United States. Amen.*

The following day, I arrived at the Consular Section of the US Embassy in Bridgetown, Barbados. I was disappointed because I thought applying for the visa would take a few hours. Instead, it took more than five days to process everything. I had to pick up the DS-160 Nonimmigrant Visa Application form, fill out the forms and include the visa fees, return all that information to the embassy and request a date for the interview, wait patiently for someone to call by phone to invite me for the interview, attend the interview and hope and pray

---

40. Celina DeCastro, "This Day in History: Regan Announces Caribbean Basin Initiative," Caribbean National Weekly, https://www.caribbeannationalweekly.com/this-day-in-history/day-history-regan-announces-caribbean-basin-initiative/.

that I passed the interview and, finally, receive a call that I needed to pick up my stamped passport.

Several days had passed since I received the news of my mom's passing. Obtaining a nonimmigrant visa from Barbados immigration was proving to be tenuous at best. It was more bothersome to obtain than I had thought. I felt annoyed and anxious.

One evening I called Cousin Eunice to give her an update on my visa application that would enable me to travel from Barbados to America. She expressed her concern that the process was taking too long. God pulled me through, and a few days later, I called her to let her know that I had succeeded.

The following week, I set out on my journey to join my bereaved dad, Nola, and the rest of my relatives. My flight from Barbados to Miami took three hours and 42 minutes. I must have fallen asleep at some point during the flight.

My Arrival in the United States

Defining life moments are the ones that leave an imprint on our hearts. This moment, arriving in America, was one of those moments. As we began our descent, hovering over the runway and then coasting toward the gate of the Miami International Airport, I quickly peered through the narrow window. The sight that greeted me was magnificent! The view of the city lights seemed to be darting and dancing along a wide floating planet as far as the eyes could see. The soft cooing of a baby or the hushed tones of some passengers signified this almost holy moment. We were all witnessing reflections as the tip of the airplane wings lighted the path to display more blues, shades of orange, white then green lights—sometimes in the shape of crosses, then butterflies. There were shimmering waves of yellow lights, then dark patches of lights darted across my field of vision like raindrops across a dark roof. Then the airplane nosed downward, a bump of wheels hitting the tarmac, and we saw the view of the airport in all its splendor! We had arrived safely.

"Welcome to Miami. Please remain in your seats. On behalf of American Airlines, thank you for flying with us. . . ."

I transited to catch the connecting flight to New Orleans, Louisiana. This time, my flight took two hours and five minutes from Miami to New Orleans.

As the aircraft descended, I could feel the familiar pain in my ear return. I hastily rummaged through my purse for two pieces of cotton balls, now tucked away in a corner of my handbag. My long-awaited dream was about to come through. The airplane was just about to touch down at the New Orleans International Airport and I was about to have my first view of New Orleans in June of 1983.

It was night. It was pitch dark outside my window and I began to feel a sense of dread. The questions flooded my mind again. *Why did this have to happen so early in her life? Did she experience lots of pain in the end? God, why did you have to take her so soon? How are my baby sister and dad taking this loss? What would life be like for my dad after more than a quarter of a century of them being together?* I would soon find out.

"Welcome to New Orleans! Please keep your seatbelts on. . . ."

My Cousin Eunice and others were waiting to take me home to Slidell from the airport. I asked how everyone was and she broke the news, "Caryl, we are sorry, we had to bury Cousin Walterine last weekend. We could not afford to keep the body any longer."

I could not speak. I would never see my mom again, and now I wasn't there in time to say goodbye. I sat silently for the duration of the journey home to Slidell. For the next month, I could not speak without crying my eyes out. I remained in that fodder for a while. I felt hopelessly floored.

When we lose loved ones too soon, we all run through the dreams we had for their lives. Even though we cannot bring the dreams we have to fruition, it doesn't mean it isn't hard to let go of the things that will never be.

Have you lost someone close to you before? What was your dream for them?

My dreams for my mother went like this: *She and my dad would thrive in America. She would get the necessary medical care that she needed. She would recover, because she was still young. She would return to school to acquire new and improved skills to realize her potential and her dreams. This young middle-aged woman would finally get the opportunity to travel to various states, to visit friends and family. She would vacation in Florida and visit her friends and family in New York. She and her children would be reunited someday. She would hug me and say, "Caryl, we made it!" We would be celebrating her birthday every year. We would be cheering for and encouraging each other. She would be with me when I gave birth to my children and be the first to hold them. Her legacy of using her gifts and talents to care for her family would be passed on to the next generation.*

But now *this*! This was, for me, my bend in the road. A huge pothole that I, a rookie in the ways of dealing with loss, had to fill somehow. This disorienting haze of coping with death in my family was virgin territory. I was ill-equipped to vault this challenge alone. My other siblings were still in Guyana. As the oldest sibling in America at that time, I was left holding the bag.

Moreover, I knew I also needed to count my blessings. My father's sister and my cousins were there. They, too, had helped my parents on arrival, to cope with the newness of life in America. They had assisted my dad in navigating the machinations of dealing with the funeral homes and underwriting the costs involved in my mother's burial.

More profoundly, I could only hope that my mother's suffering was not in vain. It was risky business traveling by plane in the crippled state that she was in. She had endured the long, three-legged, tedious 10-hour journey with layover flights from Guyana to Trinidad into Miami . . . and then on to New Orleans. Her dream to travel to America, the land of opportunity, had come through. Albeit she did not live to celebrate with me, she had paved the way for her children to receive the most coveted piece of plastic in the world, the American permanent visa.

Alas, I had no recourse but to remember the good times we shared when she made life bearable for me and my siblings by creating "magic" in and around our home and village. Whether in her modest two-room hut, the two-storied "big" house that my father, Howell, painstakingly carved out of Greenheart wood, she made all things beautiful. Like the skillful craftswoman she was, or the beautiful wedding cakes she designed, or the healing she brought to the bodies and souls of people in her sphere of influence, my mother, Walterine, will live in infinity in my thoughts and in the retelling of the stories of her life. As for me, in my mind, she still remains the first love of my heart!

That grief and resilience had to reside together in my soul. No one ever built a legacy by standing still. I had work to do. I needed to find purpose and hope in this life. A beautiful life had suddenly ended, but I needed to manage on my own now. I did not ask for this. It's like the tide. It comes in every morning and evening. Any hopes and dreams we might build on the shores of our mind could be flattened by the waves of adversity and disappointments. But do we not continue to build for fear of the unknown?

7.

God's Provision

By faith Abraham, when he was called to go to a place he would later receive as his inheritance, obeyed and went, even though he did not know where he was going.
—HEBREWS 11:8 (NEW INTERNATIONAL VERSION)

Born Again

After several weeks of mourning, weighed down by the loss of my mom, one summer morning in 1983, I walked into my late Auntie Olga's kitchen in Slidell. She was the twin sister of my Auntie Waveney, the seamstress in Guyana.

Auntie Olga took my chin in her fingers and whispered, "Jesus loves you, Caryl. He died on the cross for Cousin Walterine and he died for you, too."

I faded into her arms and allowed her to hold me for a long time as I wept. And for the first time, memories of the messages I heard in Sunday school class in the old Anglican church resurfaced in my mind. I had started to feel God's presence.

For the next few weeks, my cousins invited me to church with them. Then one Saturday evening, my Auntie Olga and my cousins Lavera and Esther invited me to attend a Leon Patillo concert. Patillo was part of the Maranatha concert group at that time, but he seemed to be a one-man show to me.

The stage was lit up in multicolored disco lights. Smoke splashed about. Leon Patillo was dressed in loose pants and baggy looking colorful blazers. He would play the piano, then the guitar, and some other funny-looking instruments that he blew into and then played on. He wore his hair long, curly and bushy. His voice and style was similar to that of another musician I liked, the late Keith Green. I was impressed! I had never experienced anything like that. Maybe it was the sheer number of people in one place, the lights, the dynamic sounds emanating from his acoustic guitars, or the contemporary style music, but I was moved, to say the least. I listened carefully to words of the songs he sang.

Then, at the end of the concert, he asked if people would like to come on stage and pray to receive Christ in their hearts. I wanted to go down, but I was scared. Just then, my Aunt Olga was sitting to my left. There were several people packed next to her, and the whole auditorium seemed awash with people. I was afraid to stand up.

The next thing I felt was this complete stranger touching me and asking if she could help me get down there! I was ready then, because the next thing I knew, she was holding my hand and leading me to the stage. I do not remember who else got on that stage that night, but all I knew was that I repeated the prayers: *God, I have sinned. I cannot help myself. Please come into my heart, Lord Jesus! Amen!*

As I got up from my knees, I became a new woman that day in the summer of 1983! All of my depression lifted and God filled my soul with His joy! I could not get enough of God's word. I remember reading the New Testament about Jesus and all the miracles that He performed, and I asked myself, *Why didn't anyone tell me this before?* I became hungry for the Word of God. I joined several Bible studies and poured my heart and soul into learning about the Lord. I began to see people differently. I loved others, regardless of their status in life, their nationality, and most of all, I loved myself. I knew then that God cared for me. I was no longer going to be alone. He sent His Holy Spirit to be my comforter. I was no longer a slave to fear, I knew I was a child of God! My mom was dead, but I had given my life to Jesus. I was now born again.

Born again means I am capable of living in two worlds. According to Pete Briscoe, one could live for eternity while dwelling here on earth.[41] First, I needed to know the truth about who I am. I am easily lured by temptations and my desire to sin is overwhelming at times. I was still very upset at God for the loss of my mom. I missed her dearly. Being aware of this truth, I needed to be set free. How am I able to be set free?

The apostle Paul said it well. "For though we live in the world, we do not wage war as the world does. The weapons we fight with are not the weapons of the world. On the contrary, they have divine power to demolish strongholds. We demolish arguments and every pretension that sets itself up against the knowledge of God, and we take captive every thought to

---

41. Pete Briscoe, "Living for Eternity While on Earth," Bible, https://www.bible.com/reading-plans/15424-living-for-eternity-while-on-earth-by-pete-briscoe/day/1.

make it obedient to Christ" (2 Cor. 10:3–5). This means that I take hold of any suspicious thoughts and question them. I just had this thought. I'm unworthy. I do not have the ability to accomplish much in life. Is this true, Lord?

Then I prayed. *Lord, please open my eyes to your truth. I want to walk in your truth.* Then I read His word to find out what He says about me. Once I continued to practice God's presence in my daily life, things became clear to me. Today, when a thought enters my mind, as soon as I recognize that it might be a lie, I test it against what the Bible says and I determine what is truth from error.

This training and renewing of my mind were by no means an overnight thing. Since my mother had died in her late 40s, I continued to struggle with the fear of dying young. Every time I fell ill, I thought that I was going to succumb to my mother's fate. Those shadow voices in my head had to go!

To compound the issue, neither my father nor I had access to health insurance. I personally prayed every day that my dad would not get sick. It took us both a while to acquire the skill of layering during the ice-cold winter months of January and February in New Orleans. The fear of catching pneumonia and dying loomed large in my mind, and I often wondered whether my dad had that fear, but I was not about to ask him.

According to an old saying, "Life gives lemons to good people, bad people, old people. Life comes with lemons. But we don't have to suck on them." And there is also a "sister saying" in Guyana, "When life gives you lemon, make lemonade." My sister Ingrid and I "made lemonade" when we figured a way out of getting into trouble. We created new uniforms out of the old. Was there a way for me to retrieve the shattered pieces of my broken heart from loss of my mother?

I was reading my Bible one day and I came across a Scripture that changed my thought life. It was Philippians 4:8: "Finally, brothers and sisters, whatever is true, whatever is noble, whatever is right, whatever is pure, whatever is lovely, whatever is admirable—if anything is excellent or praiseworthy—think about such things."

At first, I did not get that it was possible to do this. I wrote the passage on a piece of 3 x 5 card and stuck it on my dressing table mirror. Every day I read it; I also read it whenever I thought of anything negative or half-truths. When those shadow voices, fear, shame, regrets, and the what-ifs came to paralyze me, I repeated it.

It worked!

Then I went further. I made a commitment to myself. I was no longer going to live backward but live forward. Life could be understood backward, but life has to be lived forward. I resolved to accept that when Jesus died on the cross, He did that for me and everyone else. Since He completed His job, He saved me for a purpose, so my job was to find out what that purpose is and do it.

I was fascinated to read about the life of Jesus. I read the books of Matthew, Mark, Luke, and John religiously. I was very intrigued with the series of miracles of healing of the man with leprosy, healing the Centurion's paralyzed servant by speaking the words, and healing the sick woman who touched the hem of His garment, not to mention the healing of the blind and mute and many others. Jesus seemed to defy all of the old ways of thinking.

Consider Matthew 7:1–5: "For in the same way you judge others, you will be judged, and with the measure you use, it will be measured to you." And in Matthew 5:21–22: "You have heard that it was said to the people long ago, 'You shall not murder, and anyone who murders will be subject to judgment.' But I tell you that anyone who is angry with a brother or sister will be subject to judgment.'"

What I needed was courage. I later learned that courage is trusting and believing in God in the midst of my pain. So I prayed to God for joy. And by God's grace, He delivered healing to my broken heart and placed the ability to share hugs with others like I meant it from a place of hope and joy!

I had written in my journal about a number of newfound observations:

Wholeness: *Wholeness is having all the parts together and functioning as intended, realizing that a seemingly small part of that which is not functioning can sometimes cause a great problem.*

Real Christianity: *Real Christianity is never a secondhand thing (a carried story on a repeated tale); it is a personal discovery of wholeness; it is getting all my parts together and working as God intended.*

Maturity: *Maturity is both holiness and wholeness. Holiness means recovering my true humanness and becoming more like Jesus, the only perfect human being. Holiness is not piety, righteousness, or dehumanization, it is acceptance, openness, and love, in other words, being free to be a daughter of the King.*

Each of us was created as a beautiful, complex, whole person. But because of sin we have become fragmented and broken. The parts in us that need to be mature and healthy in order to function together for wholeness are the body, mind, spirit, emotions, and our social (relational aspects) of us.

I was beginning to feel whole again.

Feeling whole was not enough. I also needed wisdom. I wrote about James 3:17 on a 3 x 5 card. "But wisdom that comes from heaven is first of all pure, then peace-loving, considerate, submissive, full of mercy and good fruit, and impartial and sincere."

In other words, a wise person is one that is full of quiet gentleness. One who is peace-loving and courteous. Someone who allows discussion and is willing to yield to others; one who is full of mercy and good deeds. One who is wholehearted and straightforward and sincere. I earnestly prayed that day that I could one day gain enough wisdom to be such a person.

Losing Mom

It was summer when Howell, Walterine, and their daughter Nola arrived in Slidell, Louisiana, where the temperature topped 95 to 100 degrees. My mom would not sit still. She would go for walks in the hot sun and then stand for hours, doing what she loved to do, cooking.

Two and a half months after their arrival, she experienced a massive heart attack and had to be rushed to the Slidell Memorial Hospital. She was in a coma and my dad had to make the difficult decision to let her go. My sister Nola was 12 years old at the time, and to this day she does not remember what happened to her mom. She was traumatized! All she remembers is that she was not allowed to go to the burial ground. She was only allowed to attend my mom's funeral service. My mom's body was buried in the ground like she always requested, no tomb. "From dust, to dust. . . ."

Work in Slidell was limited, and my dad could not find any job in the area of his expertise. He, being a builder and a construction worker, could not stand to be idle. My dad and I moved to New Orleans in search of better opportunities. We left my younger sister, Nola, with my relatives to attend Slidell High School.

Imagine not being able to find a job with medical insurance: there was no way that my dad could have afforded to take my mom to see a doctor, and my mom had had a stroke before leaving Guyana. She had run out of medicines and did not mention anything to my dad or anyone else. She had been taking medications for hypertension and had run out of that as well.

Before my father and I left Slidell, I had a plan. My newfound faith was put to the test soon after giving my life to the Lord. I thought about my situation. I was given a temporary visa when I came from Barbados to the United States. I needed to be able to find an immigration lawyer to help me sort things out. I got on my knees and prayed and asked God to find me people in New Orleans who could help me find an immigration lawyer.

Since my parents had already applied for me to immigrate to the United States with them before I was 21, they had felt certain that my family would receive permission to leave Guyana before I reached that age. However, they did not receive the immigration letter until after I had turned 21. They were told to petition for me to immigrate to the United States as a single, unmarried person. So I poured my heart out to the Lord while kneeling face down on the carpet in my cousin's living room.

Since leaving Barbados, I had developed a new taste for Christian contemporary music. I had fallen in love with the musical artists Sandy Patti and Lionel Harris, and I couldn't get enough of the late Keith Green's music. I would sing his music with his same degree of passion and fervor.

I prayed and cried out to the Lord with that same passion, asking Him to make a way for me to remain within the United States. I knew I could not return to Barbados. I did not desire to leave my father and sister to fend for themselves. I felt that they were my charge and I was now responsible for helping them during this difficult time in our lives.

A few weeks later, after we had arrived in New Orleans, I was introduced to a wonderful lady, Diane (I referred to her as Lady Diana). She was and always will be a lady. I babysat her kids while I was in college, and we became very close friends. She is White, I am Black; she was rich, I was poor, but we shared a bond that was unbroken. I watched and learned from her, how to communicate and interact with one's children. She modeled how to be a fine homemaker and a lovely, intelligent, and classy woman. We would sit for hours, discussing hard subjects like race, poverty, love, and how to study Scriptures and become better Christians. She was an excellent cook and could entertain and throw a party like none other I knew at that time. Time spent with Diane was priceless. I began to understand that no matter one's status in life, the love of God should be preeminent!

I told Diane about my immigration status and she introduced me to an immigration lawyer in New Orleans. God had answered my prayers! The lawyer explained a lot about how US immigration works. He said that because my parents had applied for me to immigrate before, I needed to lie low and stay out of trouble. "Don't end up in prison, or anything stupid like that," he said. He reassured me that I would be safe. He would take on my case, free of charge, and he would notify me when it was time for me to return to Guyana and pick up my immigration green card and reenter the United States as a green card holder.

God's Provision

Meanwhile, it was hard for me and my dad to survive in New Orleans. My dad continued to look for work but could not find a job that would give him benefits such as medical insurance. We could only afford a one-bedroom apartment. My dad and I would go out looking for work and then return, tired and exhausted. We slept on the same bed.

Many nights, my dad would lament about how he had left his important tools in his workshop back in Guyana. He said, "Caryl, I wish somebody had tol' me, America was so hard to find work. I would'a bring me tools along." I reminded him that most of his tools were too heavy to be carried in his suitcase. "Don't worry Dad, you'll find a better job soon," I assured him. But I too would reminisce about my dad's work shed.

He owned a carpenter's shed in Guyana. As a child, I loved to follow my dad into his shed, absorbing the enamelware. I loved the woody smell of sawdust as it floated to the ground, leaving a smooth finish on the Greenheart wood. I was fascinated by the variety in colors and textures of the curl patterns of the shaving from the purple heart (or crabwood), silverballi, wallaba, kabukalli, and washiba woods as I gathered the remains in the palms of my hands. These memories remained with me whenever I returned to Guyana. I marveled at the longevity of the furniture and buildings with their ornate curves made from wood native to Guyana. I would saunter around, touching each type of nail, screw, hammer, and joist, asking questions about what each tool was used for. My dad would patiently explain why and how he used each tool, what type of wood was good to do "inside" work and which were perfect for building homes and furniture.

To this day, my favorite floor, furniture, or any surface is wood. Not the pressed wood. No, the real deal. The kind of wood that my dad used to build his first home from the ground floor to the ceiling! And how appropriate . . . my father's last name was Wood.

Work for my father was like medicine to keep his body and mind alert. My dad raised his family on a shoestring budget. He raised pigs, chickens, and ducks in a small area. He planted a variety of fruit trees around the yard and planted one of the largest vegetable gardens in the neighborhood where I lived. I recall gathering the long beans (bora); dark red, purple, and light green colored eggplants; green squash, huge and green colored on the outside; pumpkins, okras, cucumbers as long as my child's arm; and watermelons, peas, and peppers.

He was also a great builder and construction worker. We lived in a one-bedroom home, but my father's desire was to build a larger home for his family on the property, in front of the "old" house. He would work all week, taking care of the animals and his garden, and then on weekends, he would recruit some of his friends to help him "raise" the foundation for the new home.

My dad never took out loans from the bank. Every month he would set aside funds to purchase building material for the construction. And slowly but surely, the building began to rise up. By the time I was in high school, the house was "half-finished."

Whenever my friends got upset with me, they would let me know in no uncertain terms that my family lived in a half-finished house. Our home was finally completed by the time I was 15. My dad painted the walls in our home in lovely colors—yellows, green, pink, or sky blue. My older sister and I got to choose a color for our bedroom, and he showed us how to carefully paint the walls of our room.

The dark brown hardwood in our living room floor shone like ivory. We had to remove our shoes at the front door before entering the living room. My dad painted the wooden steps also. We walked up and down stairs painted brown in the center and yellow on both sides. The railings on the steps were colored brown. The following year, or whenever the colors dimmed, we walked on red steps in the center with green on both sides, etc.

As wonderful as my father was, he too was a broken vessel in a number of ways. Maybe it was the fact that he never experienced normal childhood. Howell would never be found having fun on the dance floor. My dad never played soccer or entertained the thought of playing ball with his three sons. Conversations with his children were few and only to teach or correct mistakes. Our dad was a person to be admired but not someone his children wanted to spend time with.

Whenever our dad arrived from work, all playing and fun stopped. With military precision, we quickly packed our playthings away and waited for his entrance. Time spent with our dad was to work, not to play. I later learned that the recurring disagreement between him and my mom was over the fact that she, being nine years younger and full of energy, wanted to attend parties, and he refused to go with her throughout their lifetime.

As I lay next to my dad, I realized that conversation with my dad now in New Orleans, flowed easily. Growing up in

Guyana, interactions with my dad were few and far between. Most of our exchanges were about how I was doing in school or did I finish my chores. He never asked about my friends or what I thought about the political situation in the country. He always seemed deep in thought and upset about something. I did not recall ever hearing my dad laugh out loud.

Now my dad wanted to know whether I had heard from my classmates or my siblings and what my plans were for the next year now that I was in America. I told him I definitely wanted to go to college. "I heard without a degree of some sort, one cannot get ahead in this part of the world," I said empathically.

One evening, the landlord called my dad and me to discuss something that was bothering her. She said that she was concerned about the fact that my dad and I were sleeping together on the same bed. In America, she said, it is against the law for such arrangements to occur. I would have to leave and find my own apartment or both of us would need to leave and find a two-bedroom apartment.

We were both surprised to hear about this. We came from a background where survival was the name of the game. Families slept in the same room and bed to survive, until they could save enough to get ahead. Later, I would learn why it was against the law for a father and daughter to share a one-bedroom apartment and many other taboos about living life in America.

My cousins contacted some relatives of ours and they were willing to host me temporarily in their home. They were a family of four (Cousin Kristine and her husband and their two beautiful daughters, Sharon and Michelle). So my dad remained in the one-bedroom apartment and I moved in with my cousins. This was an act of love and grace bestowed on me, for which I will always be grateful. Life continued peacefully. I joined a church, attended Bible study frequently, and I continued to pray that things would get better.

My friend Diane introduced me to more friends of hers, and I would babysit for them. I remember one particular time I was working for a lady and she asked me how things were. I told her things weren't too great but that my dad and I were doing our best to make ends meet. After much probing she told me that she and her husband could help us find an apartment. They would approach their church congregation to see whether they could help us fund our rent for the first two months and they would pray that my dad would find permanent work. They kept their word, and we were able to move into a two-bedroom apartment in a nicer part of town.

So, that summer of 1984, we moved into a two-bedroom apartment in the western part of New Orleans. My dad did most of the cooking, and he was a decent cook. He had learned to survive by cooking simple meals whenever he held jobs to construct large bridges in the interior parts of Guyana. He would invite complete strangers to come have a taste of his meal.

Then things started to look even better for us. I started taking the streetcar across town to work for a couple who were both lawyers. They had a son named Jimmy. Jimmy was a fun, intelligent four-year-old boy who loved to be cuddled and read to. He loved when I read historical fiction books to him, and I personally learned a great deal about American history from reading those books to him.

My days were filled with playing with Jimmy. I watched him ride his bike in the park. In addition to reading to him, I would also put him down for naps, clean the house, and cook supper before his parents returned home. Then I would catch the streetcar and head back home. I worked five days a week and sometimes, when his parents needed to go somewhere special, I would babysit for them on weekends.

On my way to and from work, I would see the Tulane University campus, and while out and about, I would visit the New Orleans and Loyola University campuses. I soon learned from my cousins that in order to attend college, one has to study for the ACT or SAT. So I went to the bookstore and bought the *Barron's ACT Study Guide*. I studied the book diligently, and whenever I had questions, I asked my friends for clarification. I found out where the test centers were in New Orleans and I took the test. I requested that my scores be sent to all the major four-year universities in the city and waited patiently for my scores. My scores came back and I had done reasonably well. I was not aware that one could take the test many times over, but I applied to the universities and got accepted to the University of New Orleans and somewhere else. I was so excited!

Then reality hit me. I could not afford the tuition to go to school and I was not eligible to apply for financial aid. Thus, I began to pray to the Father to help me get my green card before the fall of 1985. I knew it was a tall order, but by then, I had increased my faith and I had no recourse; there only one to whom I could turn to for a miracle. I accepted admission to the University of New Orleans on faith. I sent in everything that I needed to and waited on the Lord.

Have you ever been waiting so long for things to come together and you just don't know if that is the path you are meant to be on? It felt like so much waiting. Then, the "miracle call" came through.

In March of 1984, I received the telephone call from the lawyer's office that my green card was ready to be picked up. One has to travel outside of the United States and then return through Miami or New York to make the official entrance. I chose to return to Guyana. I was so happy! I called all my friends from my church who had been praying for me, and we celebrated like I had won the lottery. I had won the most coveted ticket to success that the world knew then, a chance to obtain permanent residency status in America!

Returning to the United States from Guyana was with the peace that we now had the chance to keep moving forward with life. However, we were still troubled about the rental issue and the fact that my dad was still not able to find full-time employment. My dad had applied to several places for work, but nothing ever seemed to come up.

Crawfish Boil

Every American city that I have lived in has its traditional festival and unique culture. These festivals normally focus on celebrating the food, music, and arts and crafts as well as the history of the people who reside in those cities. In Guyana, it is the annual Mashramani (MASH) Celebration in recognition of Guyana becoming a republic in 1970. This event is usually held on February 23.[42] In Barbados, it is the Crop Over Festival, which lasts for three months and ends with a grand carnival.[43]

42. "Mashramani," Wikipedia, https://en.wikipedia.org/wiki/Mashramani.
43. "The Barbados Crop Over Festival," Visit Barbados, https://visitbarbados.org/crop-over-festival.

There are a vast number of festivals year-round in Chicago; however, the Taste of Chicago" known as the "The Taste" is one of my favorites. It is considered one of the world's largest food festival and lasts for five days in July at Grant Park.[44]

Springfield boasts many opportunities to showcase its talents and culture. Apart from being home to the Abraham Lincoln Museum and the annual State Fair held in August each year, the biggest downtown outdoor festival is held in late September.[45]

Throughout my time in New Orleans, I have spent many weekends touring the famous French Quarter, Bourbon Street, and I've even participated in Mardi Gras. The annual crawfish boil is a Louisiana tradition, which lasts the longest and has spread to nearby states like Texas and other southern states. The crawfish (known as crawdads) peak season is during March to mid-June and another from mid-November through mid-August. I think I prefer it, because crawfish boil is a family and feasting time in New Orleans. Restaurants prepare months ahead to host sometimes over 200 people at a time to hold crawfish boils and people are encouraged to "eat all you can." Some restaurants hold contests to see who can eat the most within a certain time. People have been known to consume over 6,000 pounds of crawfish per day at some restaurants over Memorial Day. Crawfish boil is also held in

---

44. "Taste of Chicago," Wikipedia, https://en.wikipedia.org/wiki/Taste_of_Chicago#:~:text=The%20Taste%20of%20Chicago%20(known,the%20largest%20festival%20in%20Chicago.
45. A Google search for "Largest Festival In Springfield, Illinois" generated over two million results.

private homes and at special end-of-year gathering on campuses all over New Orleans.[46]

You know how sometimes you see things every day, but it never really hits you what it means? I had seen the "Crawfish Crossing" sign, but I never *really* saw it. You know, like the speed limit on Main Street in your neighborhood that says "45 miles an hour." You never knew it said that until the police showed it to you while giving you a speeding ticket.

I remember first seeing crawdads on the side of the road near Lake Pontchartrain. Yes, vehicles were piling up behind as we stopped because there were several of these things crawling across the road. So could you imagine what it sounded like when my college friends invited me to a crawfish boil?

It was a weekend and they seemed very excited.

"June, let's go!"

I asked, "Where? What is a crawfish boil?"

"It's a party and we get to eat as much as we like. I can't wait!"

I cringed on the inside but I said, "Wow! How does it taste?"

They all looked at me like I was crazy.

"You never tasted crawfish?"

I explained that the only seafood I eat is shrimp, crab, and fish. I do not like mussels or anything that I have to lick off a shell. They reassured me that I would like crawfish. They said in unison, "They are delicious!"

And off we went.

---

46. "Crawfish, Crayfish, Crawdad – It's the Season in New Orleans," Free Tours by Foot, https://freetoursbyfoot.com/crawfish-new-orleans/#:~:text=It%20 is%20crayfish%20time%20in,%2DNovember%20through%20mid%2DAugust.

We arrived at the home of one of the University of New Orleans students. We walked on the side of the home then turned the corner, and what confronted me next was, to say the least, fascinating. There was a long white tent over what must have been several long tables joined together. The tables were covered with white wax-like paper. Several people were standing around talking and drinking beer, soft drinks, water, etc. At one end of the tables stood three people armed with giant mesh ladles and scoops. They were working over a giant pot set on a fire source attached to a gas propane bottle.

Whatever they were making needed lots of everything: There were huge bottles of seasonings. I edged closer to see. There were giant-sized bottles of Zatarain's® Shrimp and Crab Boil Liquid, large bottles of hot sauce, garlic powder, ground cayenne pepper, salt, and lemon extract. Then there were a variety of other ingredients lying around: bags of bay leaf, bowls of triangle-shaped cut lemons, jalapeño pepper, sticks of butter, stalks of celery and onions cut into bite-sized cubes, fresh garlic, small whole and cut red potatoes, and half pieces of corn on the cub. I noticed they had some whole crabs and shrimp, but there was also the dreaded sight of snails still encased in their shells. I cringed at the sight of those, but then I also saw large cuts of sausage. There were huge bags of ice sitting under the table. I figured that the snails would be easy to pick out before I ate the rest of my meal.

I watched them pour seasoning into the boiling water and add the butter and other ingredients while stirring everything with their huge ladles and spoons. Then I left to visit with my friends. There were people from the neighborhood. I met many others from campus, relatives of the host family and their young children. This crawfish boil was indeed a family affair. I think I felt very at home in that kind of atmosphere, and soon enough, the next thing I heard was that it was time to eat.

I walked over to the tent and the smell and sight assailed my senses! It took four people to lift and scatter huge globs of cascading multi-colored edibles. The dark-red curled crawfish tumbled out of the pot, their dark eyes bulging as some seemed to cling to each other for security. Along with the bright yellow corn, green beans, and pink potatoes, I saw the black shell of the snails, the brown with pink insides of the sausage, and plenty of lemons. This created a rainbow of colors set against the now greasy white of the "tablecloth." The smell of hot pepper blended with savory spices and mouthwatering juices was an arresting experience to behold.

Someone asked whether anyone needed to learn how to shell and eat the crawfish. A few of us raised our hands and we were shown how to break part of the head off the body. Then we were tutored to suck the head and break the top two rings of the crawfish to eat the meat off. After a few unsuccessful attempts, I got the hang of it.

Eating crawfish is messy but fun. The flavor of the meat is similar to that of crab and shrimp together. It turned out to be a very satisfying experience for me, and for many years, I, like many others, embraced the New Orleans French-based cuisine of the crawfish boil!

Interestingly, after that first experience, I was hooked! My dad and I were invited to another crawfish boil. As usual, we were the only two minority people in the room except a tall, dark, and handsome gentleman. He smiled when he saw us enter the room and came over to greet us. He extended his right hand.

"Hi, I'm Courtney Blair, and you are?"

"I am June. And this is my father, Howell Wood," I said, while gesturing toward my father. After my father said hello, Mr. Blair rolled his eyes and declared, "You all are Guyanese!" His whole posture changed then. He, too, was a Guyanese immigrant.

We continued our conversation as we reminisced about life lived in Guyana. Later, he introduced us to several new people, including some who taught at Loyola University. He was a professor. During our conversation, we told him about Dad's work situation. He encouraged my dad to go to the university and fill out an application. According to the professor, they were hiring people to work as maintenance workers.

The Interview

My dad applied for the job, and several weeks later they called him for an interview. We were very excited! After several interviews and assurances, they called him in to get fitted for his work clothes to begin work the following week. My dad appeared as requested and was ready to start the following Monday. On Saturday, he received a call from the foreman, who was not there when my dad had interviewed for the position. He said, "Mr. Wood, there was a mistake. You should not come to work on Monday as planned. That position has been filled already."

My dad was heartbroken, of course. After some time, we called the professor and told him what had happened. He was silent on the phone and then muttered under his breath, "I cannot believe they are playing this game again." Then he said to my dad, "Mr. Wood, you don't return anything. I'll take care of things."

So my dad and I prayed and waited for a call from the professor. However, the call never came from the professor. Instead, the following Monday morning, my dad received a call from someone else. It was the same person who had called before on the phone. He said, "Mr. Wood, I am calling to apologize. There was a mistake. Please come to work as you had planned on doing." So my dad quickly got dressed and showed up for work. He never looked back!

My father showed up for work as a maintenance worker at Loyola University, armed with the same forces that he depended on throughout his lifetime: the desire to work hard and take responsibility for completing whatever tasks were assigned to him. And just like he did in Guyana, rain or shine, my dad performed his duties with dignity and pride. He knew that he had finally obtained his dream of coming to America, the land of the free, the home of the brave. He paved the way for his family to escape poverty. Not only did he desperately need that job to earn money to help his family, the church had only agreed to pay our rent for two months. Without a steady income, we would not have been able to afford to live in that apartment. Moreover, we needed some form of health insurance coverage, and Loyola University provided that assurance for their full-time employees.

One evening my dad returned from work, grinning from ear to ear.

"Caryl, I worked on the roof today. Those guys were laughing when the boss told me to climb up there and fix the gutter on the roof. They don't know how many roofs I climbed in my lifetime. They tink me too old . . . I showed them!"

My father worked diligently for seven years before he retired from Loyola University. He won awards for his hard work and dedication. Years after his retirement from Loyola University, he hung the framed 12 x 14 photo of the university community on the walls of his home in Friendship Village. It became a conversation piece for visitors and family. He was proud of his accomplishments.

Professor Blair is also among the people in that framed 12 x 14 photo. He not only taught at Loyola University but also touched the lives of numerous students when he taught at Dillard and Xavier universities. He was a strong advocate for students. He sacrificed his time to tutor and mentor many. He stood for truth and fairness and justice. He was always ready to go the extra mile to ensure justice was done. That same spirit is what led Professor Blair to stand up for what was right when my dad was being discriminated against. I read of his departure from this earth at the age of 60 in January 2009. I will always remember him for his courage to defend my dad when he needed to.

"For though we live in the world, we do not wage war as the world does. The weapons we fight with are not the weapons of the world. On the contrary, they have divine power to demolish strongholds. We demolish arguments and every pretension that sets itself up against the knowledge of God, and we take captive every thought to make it obedient to Christ"

—2 Cor. 10:3–5

8.

New Orleans Campus Life

I leave you a thirst for education. Knowledge is the prime need of the hour. If I have a legacy to leave my people, it is my philosophy of living and serving.
—MARY JANE MCLEOD BETHUNE, EDUCATOR AND FOUNDER OF DAYTONA NORMAL & INDUSTRIAL INSTITUTE FOR NEGRO GIRLS, DAYTONA, FLORIDA

Many of us have forged ahead through education and can re-count the different hurdles we faced to reach the other side. The University of New Orleans (UNO) holds a special place in my heart. Not only because of its academic rigor or national stature but also because it provided an average student, a poor immigrant like me, the opportunity to learn about myself and to navigate a new territory of learning how to learn.

When I first started attending the University of New Orleans (UNO) in 1985, I felt like a fish out of water. I was unfamiliar with the rhythm of campus life at first, but I soon learned the art of scheduling every waking moment of my life.

My first day of class, during roll call, I heard the name, "June Wood." I looked around the room to see who had the same last name as I. I was accustomed to being called "Caryl" all my life while growing up in Guyana. Everyone knew me as Caryl back then, so for a moment I did not respond. I soon embraced the name and the sound of it. Every important correspondence I received from college addressed me as June Wood. I had become "June."

UNO was also the perfect climate for nontraditional students like me (older) or working and part-time students and parents. Most of all, unlike the other institutions, it was very racially diverse. My classmates were from Asia, the Caribbean, India, and Africa. We enjoyed participating in the annual International Student Gala. Students showcased the colorful clothing from their homeland. We feasted on a variety of tasty ethnic foods and enjoyed listening to—and sometimes dancing to—upbeat music.

Because I was eligible for financial aid, I was able to attend college full time and, to my amazement, got a work-study job for a total of 15 hours a week on campus. I felt like I had won the lottery again, twice in a row! I got a job working in the International Student Office under the leadership of the director of that office. I still remember she attended my wedding years later. I was very impressed that she would do such a thing. I enjoyed working with international students from India, China, Peru, Germany, Australia, Britain, and other nations. This job allowed me to interact with several students from diverse parts of the world.

I assisted students with information on obtaining their 1-20 Forms. The 1-20 Form, also known as the "Certificate of Eligibility for Nonimmigrant (F-1) Students," allows them to attend vocational schools, colleges, and universities in the United States. I booked spaces on campus for students to hold their fraternity, sorority, and other meetings. I provided important information and resources for students to learn English and succeed academically. I also counseled students on when and how to sign up for and add or drop classes before the deadline.

Occasionally, my boss invited me to participate in immigration-related discussions with the university administrators. She felt that because I was an immigrant, I might lend some insight into what course of action was best for students. She had a calm, gentle persona, yet she relentlessly fought for the UNO administration to address issues and enact polices in favor of international students.

Being a student was easy for me, and I poured myself into studying all kinds of subjects. However, there were many things that I needed to learn about the college system. It took me a while to master the lingo of the college life. I learned about first and second period, free period, credits per hour, majors and minors, "get tutoring," and the importance of an excellent grade-point average. Originally, I was all over the place when it came to "majoring in something." I asked my best friend, Carol, at the time, "What is majoring?" She said, "You have to go to your advisor and get advice on what courses are available to take in your study of interest."

One semester, I had registered for five classes and was juggling studies, work, and my social life. I ended up with three Cs. That brought my grade point average down from a B to a C. I went to see my English teacher and she looked at my academic records. She was concerned and encouraged me to only take four classes per semester and work on bringing up my grade point average.

I learned to manage my schedule better, and after I got married in my senior year of college, I discovered something amazing! I had never consistently studied in a quiet, undisturbed atmosphere before. So, most evenings, after my husband and I ate dinner, we returned to his work environment at Louisiana State University. I sat for hours, in the quiet of the main-framed computer lab, pouring over my textbooks, underlining and interacting with the information on the pages. When exam time came, I felt like the answers to the questions jumped out of my mind. I began to ace every test. I had finally discovered the skill of learning how to learn! I graduated in 1989 with a Bachelor of Education degree and obtained my Teacher Certification.

One of My Favorite Places on Campus

As you can imagine, I grew to love the University of New Orleans campus. My favorite view was that of the northern part of the university campus. The university is located in a very beautiful part of the city. It is close to the Lake Pontchartrain Beach and the Lake Terrace. It is rightly dubbed the "Lakefront Campus."

I spent most of my time in the education wing. Every time I looked out from the third floor of the College of Education building, the scene was fantastic! Looking over the cove was a treat to anyone who loves nature. At seven o'clock in the morning on a clear day before the hustle and the bustle of student activities begins, the lawns appeared to be resting quietly under the shade of trees and plants. Everywhere, everything seemed to be at rest, and even the chirping sound of birds was subdued, as though there was an unspoken rule among them: "Be quiet!" The birds seemed to be enjoying this part of the day before the unending flow of student and faculty footsteps began to invade their space. They alighted gently from bush to grass, lifted their heads in search of sounds and persons, then settled down again.

The houses along the lake were mostly modern ranch-style buildings, compared to the older parts of the city where shotgun homes and palaces abounded. These homes appeared to be tucked in and almost hidden by the sprawling trees. Above the treetops the sky had a soft, yellowish hue mingled with the blues and grays. In the distance, when evening came, the streetlights added to the beauty of the scenery. The lights looked like small yellow stars dotting the atmosphere. By 7:45 a.m., there were a number of familiar sounds in the air around the campus buildings. There was the clanging sound of the elevator, and the sight of a cleaner, clad in gloves and outerwear, bucket and brush in hand. She had completed her chores of dusting, wiping, and cleaning.

A walk across campus from that building could be very tedious, but thanks to the gardeners, every portion of land was well taken care of. This truly was landscaping of its purest form—not a blade of grass was out of place! The green plants and colorful flowers created a picturesque view for students as they passed by, and the burden of tramping around campus was lessened by the beauty of the surroundings.

Traveling by Bus in True American Style

Traveling to and from college by bus can be very interesting. Unlike my experience of taking the bus in Barbados, there are subtle differences in doing so in New Orleans. In New Orleans you get to the bus stop on time and the bus does not come until 10 or 15 minutes later. Other times you arrive just as the bus pulls off.

If the bus stop is at a transfer point, there is usually a constant flow of people joining you in your wait for your bus. Some would arrive and leave quickly because they were fortunate to be taking a bus that ran on schedule. The others would remain, and if the bus comes three minutes later, there is hardly any conversation. Everyone tries his or her best to avoid looking at the other. If the bus still does not arrive, everyone automatically directs his or her attention to the other and makes some sort of comment about the bus being late, "all the time."

After traveling on the bus for a while, you will eventually recognize most of the people (the regulars) who travel with you, but the same attitude will prevail each day. People will always pretend not to know each other until everyone is faced in a situation of stress or anxiety. People rarely speak loudly on the bus. The bus is a good place to read and catch up on one's homework. It is also a pleasant place to take a nap. The constant droning of the engine can cause you to drift off to sleep.

One day a lady got on the bus and she did not stop speaking. Everyone looked at her in awe. Some people looked embarrassed too. Eventually she got off the bus, and I could actually feel and hear the sigh of relief as she did so. The rest of the ride appeared to be very traditional. Another time, three young men got on the bus. One look at them told me that they did not ride the bus often. First, their conversation was very loud. Second, they looked directly at everyone that was on the bus, and third, they began to use profane language back and forth to each other.

Soon the bus came to a stop and I immediately recognized the danger. The bus driver firmly assured them that if he heard more "crap" from them, they would be thrown off the bus. The young men looked rather astonished, and for the next five minutes not a sound was heard coming from them. Soon they were chatting with each other in much lower tones. They had finally adjusted to the norms of people who ride on the bus.

My First Car

Now that my father and I lived out in the "suburbs," I suddenly had the urge to own a car of my own. I had saved enough money to purchase my own vehicle, I thought. So I asked a friend who knew about vehicles to join me in the search. I had rehearsed in my mind the kind of vehicle that I saw myself driving. It had to be red, of course, not too big, something with four doors. I hated getting into those cars with two doors, where I felt like I had to do gymnastics before entering the vehicle.

It was the summer of 1985, and I needed a vehicle to get to and from college. I had saved a total of $1,000 toward this venture, and I was not going to leave the car lot without my dream car. The fall semester was about to begin, and I wanted to be ready. I had taken the driving classes and I had my driver's license intact.

To my surprise, we spent hours walking down the narrowing aisles of the used car parking lots and could not find anything near my price range. I felt dejected and disgusted. Then the used car dealer probably felt sorry for me. He beckoned us over, saying, "Here's a nice one in your price range!"

We hurried over and leaned in. It was a dark brown 1977 Toyota Corolla. It had four doors and appeared a bit banged up on one side. The price was right under my budget, but there was one other problem. It was a manually operated transmission (stick shift) car. I had never driven one before!

I bought the car, and by the time I had paid for all the essential registration and such, the total came to around $950. My friend drove the car to our apartment and parked it on the street. The challenge was that school was about to start in two weeks. How do I learn to drive a stick shift in two weeks?

One morning after church, a friend asked how the car shopping went. I told her my problem. She declared, "I can teach you how to drive your car!" I asked her if she was serious and she said, "Yes, I'll come by your house and pick you up. I know a park by my parents' home that is good for that sort of training." She spent several days teaching me until I felt comfortable behind the wheel.

One day after driving lessons, she said, "June, that's my home over there." She pointed across the street in the direction of a pale-brown brick ranch-style home. "You play ping-pong, right?" she asked. I answered, "I sure do. I played for my high school in Guyana. I might be a bit rusty now."

She invited me to her home to play. Her parents were home. She rang the doorbell and her dad answered the door. I reached out my hand to shake her dad's hand and he turned away and went back inside.

Throughout my visit that day, I never saw her parents again. I asked my friend what that was about. She replied, "My parents have never interacted with Black people and they don't want to do so now." I thought to myself, *I think I'm a harmless person. I wonder why they did not even try to get to know me before making their decision about me. Did people of color hurt them in the past?* My friend reassured me, "I'm working on my parents." I wondered what she meant by that, but I did not ask her.

Whatever it was that affected my friend's parent, I was happy that she was over that. I realized that day, that James Baldwin's thoughts on victimhood were correct: "Perhaps the turning point in one's life is to realize that to be treated like a victim is not necessarily to become one."[47]

I learned a lesson that day.

Driving Lessons Two

I remembered that evening like it was yesterday: I was wearing my blue jeans and black three-quarter sleeve button-down shirt and my familiar red belt and red suspenders. The sun was setting in the sky. The pinkish-reds were chasing the yellow skyline against the darkness of evening light. I said to my dad, "Dad, I think I know how to drive my car now. Do you want to go for a ride with me?" He said, "Okay."

We both got in the car, him sitting in the passenger seat and me in the driver's seat. I put my foot on the accelerator. To this day, I do not know what saved us. The car shot forward, missing the telephone post on the side of the road by inches, and stopped with a jerk! Our bodies slumped forward and then back in our seats in unison. We stared at each other. My dad did not say a word. I apologized profusely, "Dad, I'm soo sorry!" I sat in the car. I replayed the scene in my mind to see

---

47. McKenzie Jean-Phillipe, "35 Poignant James Baldwin Quotes on Love and Justice That Are Especially Timely," *Oprah Magazine,* June 12, 2020, https://www.oprahmag.com/life/g32842156/james-baldwin-quotes/?slide=25.

what I had done wrong. "Aha!" I had figured out what I had done wrong.

I finally picked up the courage to try driving my car again, and I did so successfully for the duration of my college years at the University of New Orleans. I had wonderful times of worship and prayers in that car. After my husband and I got married in 1988, we were able to purchase a small Toyota Tercel. My dad was able to use that brown Toyota Corolla to go to work whenever he did not take the streetcar.

*Photo of the late
Walterine Wood*

*Photo of Walterine Wood
(before she left Guyana)*

*Photo of the late
Howell Wood*

*Left to Right: Lennox, Ru-
dolph, Elroy, Ingrid,
June, and Nola*

Buxton Village Main Road

Friendship Main Road

*Buxton Government Secondary School, Friendship Village,
where June started high school*

Home of the late Dr. Hope next to June's home on Friendship Road

The tradition of June's dad: Howell's colorful steps

This is me when I first arrived in Barbados. I'm standing on the front porch of the residence where I stayed.

June next to her first car

*This is me by the apart-
ment where my dad and
I lived on Stroelitz Street
in New Orleans.*

*Two medical
students bowed
down to us after
our wedding in New
Orleans.*

*June's first trip to Ghana in the early 1990s
with her husband, Dr. Edem Agamah*

*June and Dr. Edem Agamah in front of
IHDN Mission Hospital, Weta, Ghana*

*June received the University of Illinois
Humanitarian Award in 2014.*

June and her family at the award ceremony

*June and Dr. Agamah received the State
Journal Registrar honor for Finalist for the
Legacy in Healthcare Award in 2015.*

Our daughters, Aseye, Miriam, and Sarah

*My Cousin Errol and Vashti Cockfield have
been a great support to me over the years.
Cousin Vashti's cooking reminds me of my
mother's cooking in Guyana.*

*June and her tennis
buddy, Valerie*

*June in New York
decked out in her
Ghanaian dress wear*

June and her daughters visit family in New York

June and her daughters visited with family and friends in Georgetown, Guyana.

June and her daughters visited the amazing Kaieteur Falls, one of the world's largest cascading waterfalls.

The Schultz family also visited Guyana.

The late Dr. Montague (Monty) Hope, Howell Wood, and the pastor of the Anglican Church in Friendship

My daughters were able to meet my best friend Monty's daughters during our visit to Guyana.

9.

Taking Risks and Resting in God's Promises

*We are not valuable because of the color of our skin,
the job we do, our position in life, or our wealth,
but we are valuable just because we are intrinsically
made in the image of God.*
—ANONYMOUS

So many times we all face moments where we have to make a decision that may result in huge changes. For me, a series of events occurred in my journey that helped me make the major decisions in my life. It is risky business to leave familiar things.

When I left Guyana, I had left behind the culture I grew up in, my family and friends, familiar foods, a lifestyle I was accustomed to, and my language. I was willing to start all over again. I am a living witness, a woman who took a leap of faith and trusted in the God who created the universe. The One who created me, made life bearable, sometimes even hopeful, under the most difficult of times.

There were times when I personally wanted to give up because there seemed to be no way around or above my circumstances. I gained the strength to press on. God removed obstacles from my path and brought me to my appointed goal. You may say, "Why? Why should you take the risk?"

I would like to suggest three reasons why you should trust God. First, God's eyes continually see our past. Second, God's eyes continually see our present situation, and third, God's eyes continually see our future. God reminded me of Jeremiah 31:3: "The Lord appeared to us in the past, saying: 'I have loved you with an everlasting love; I have drawn you with unfailing kindness.'" It reaffirms that He *really sees me*!

God Sees Me

I recalled an incident that occurred in 1986 at a retreat in Florida for single adults that were interested in getting married. Friends from my church invited me to attend the retreat. I was then attending a predominantly White church. That summer, someone invited a young African American man, Greg Harris, to the church. As usual, I was asked to "reach out" to him. I took on the challenge and asked him whether he would like to accompany me to the retreat. At first, he said, "No." Later, he confessed, "I feel uncomfortable hanging out with White people because of the history of race relations in America." I reassured him that if he went with me, he would be okay. Throughout our time there, he remained skeptical and felt like we were being *tolerated*.

Greg and I were relaxing outside the hotel. We sat facing each other as we watched the waves lick the shoreline and recede back into the ocean. Then he remarked, "June, I know you were not born here. Let me tell you, here in America,

Black people are not welcomed in White people's circles. You will never be accepted. They just tolerate you because you come around them."

There it was again—the *race* issue.

I told him, "That may be true, but I think God has a plan. Maybe if more people like you and I get with God's agenda, then America might experience the greatest racial reconciliation in our churches. Then could you imagine what would happen when that spills out from the church into society?"

He looked at me and shook his head. Soon it was time to join the others in the conference room. We headed across the street and entered a large room and, of course, he and I were the only people of color there. What happened next reassured me that God does see me.

The leader introduced himself and his wife. Then he said, "Lets pray before we start. God has laid the topic of racial reconciliation on my heart." He then suggested, "Let's break up in groups of five. We will remain in our groups for the rest of the evening."

At the end of his prayer, he said, "The Lord has a message for someone in this room."

As soon as he said that, my right ear physically opened up like someone opening a tap. Like a mother turning her child's ear in the direction of the sound of his voice, I heard the message loud and clear. *He watched over me from childhood. He knows the desires of my heart. He has a plan and purpose for my life. I needed to be patient, for He has someone "special" for me.*

As soon as the message was over, my ear returned to normal. I was shocked! The God of the universe saw me and made His presence felt in that room full of strangers!

That was my Hagar moment. Hagar was Sarai's young handmaiden that gave birth to Abraham's son, Ishmael. God confronted her as she fled from her home. He told her that she should return home because she is pregnant. The place where God confronted her, was at a Spring, named *Beer Lahai Roi* (You are the God who sees me" [Gen. 16:1–16]).

Psalm 139:13–16 became clear to me that day. "For you created my innermost being; you knit me together in my mother's womb. I praise you because I am fearfully and wonderfully made; your works are wonderful, I know that full well. My frame was not hidden from you when I was made in the secret place, when I was woven together in the depths of the earth. Your eyes saw my unformed body, all the days ordained for me were written in your book before one of them came to be."

The sound of those words resounded in my being because I knew God saw me in Friendship Village. He was with me when as a little girl: I would twirl around and around as I looked up to the clear blue skies and yearned to know whether He was up there in the sky. Then, I would grow dizzy. I'd stop, feeling the world spin out of control. Then I'd fall to the ground.

He saw me when I disobeyed my parents and my girlfriend and I snuck into the garden to pick pretty red peppers with my bare hands. I suffered from the pepper burns silently for three days after washing myself. Yes, God saw me in that village, a poor carpenter's daughter, singing her Sunday school songs at the top of her lungs in the kitchen with a tattered roof.

He said, "She is mine!" For He created my innermost being. "He knit me in my mother's womb."

And this is exactly what God wants to do in each of our hearts. He sees the hungry child in the village. He aches with the young mother who yearns to hear encouraging words from her husband. He knows that you are afraid to risk surrendering your future to Him. However, He is the One who knows and sees you. God knows about you. He sees your past and your future. He has a plan and a purpose for your life. After all, He is our Creator!

Edem's Story

Of all the risks that I have taken, the greatest risk was to marry my husband, Edem.

He grew up in a middle-class family in Ghana, West Africa. Our home countries may sound the same, but West Africa is a very different place. He is the second-born child but the first-born male child in a family of four (two boys and two girls). His dad was a bank manager and his mother combined home-making with trading in cloth and other household goods. Despite his upbringing, he experienced some of the difficulties that came with rural and village life.

When he was in high school, his father built a two-story home in the village of Agbozume, in the Volta Region of Ghana. Edem attended Keta Secondary School, but throughout his summer vacation, he spent his time in Agbozume, studying, planting, and tending a vegetable garden.

In those days, in 1971, electricity was scarce but his family was fortunate to have access to a generator, which provided power. The villagers had access to water from a public tap. When the tap was turned off, they had to carry water in a bucket from the well. He was fully aware of poverty and prayed that he would do well in boarding school. It was in boarding school that Edem gave his life to the Lord. After attending secondary school, he was fortunate to get into medical school and move to Accra, Ghana.

Edem was a planner, and he told his mom that he would like to meet someone and get married and start a family after medical school. He completed medical school at the age of 25 and quickly discovered that he was the youngest graduate in his cohort. He was unable to meet the right person to marry. He remembers praying to God, asking Him, *Why is it that on the planet Earth, there is no Christian woman suitable for me?*

In 1987, he came to Louisiana State Medical School on the New Orleans campus to pursue a graduate degree in biostatistics. One of his pressing concerns was whether he would ever find someone who was right for him, especially in a new culture and environment. He was active in a predominantly White church, the Berean Bible Church, on the Westbank of New Orleans. He did not own a car, so he had to take public transportation into New Orleans and back home from school every day. This prevented him from interacting or socializing much with people apart from his church community. So his meeting me was the least likely event based on human analysis. We lived on two separate sides of town. I lived in New Orleans and also attended an Assemblies of God church. Like me, he was the only Black person attending that church at the time.

June's Story

When I was a senior at the University of New Orleans, I received a telephone call from my friend Diana. We had attended church together in 1984 and had lost touch with each other. She informed me that she got my number from another of our mutual friends. She wanted to contact me because, as she said, "I'm attending the same church with a really nice young physician. He is from your country, Ghana." I politely told her, "Diana, I am not from Ghana. I am from Guyana, South America." She said, "Oh my, I'm so embarrassed! I thought you were from Ghana."

She went on to describe how she had met Edem several times because he hung out with another friend, Rick. She continued, "Edem is a nice guy, you should meet him. Can I give him your number?" We ended the conversation after catching up on things. She was then attending the Berean Bible Church and enjoying it very much.

I took my first risk that day: I told her yes.

For the next few months, Edem and I must have called and spoken to each other daily. He said he loved the Lord, and we seemed to share many things in common. Like me, he wanted to be used of the Lord to be an instrument of change in the world, but we both did not have a clue how. We would often share Scriptures, talk about our families, and pray on the phone about and for each other. We would always end the conversation by saying, "We should meet sometime."

Edem and I finally met one evening. It was a Friday night. A group of friends from my church and I planned to attend a free concert by a contemporary singing group. They planned to meet at a coffee house in New Orleans East.

During our conversation, I asked Edem whether he would like to go with us. He said, "Yes, but I have no way to get there. I don't have a car."

I offered to pick him up from LSU Medical School Center, but we had a problem. We did not know what each other looked like. There were no smartphones in those days.

I asked, "What do you look like?"

He answered, "I'm short. I have a big head."

"What are you wearing?" I asked.

He answered, "I'm wearing a light brown and cream short-sleeved shirt and some light brown khaki pants. I'll be carrying a brown briefcase."

I thought to myself, *Who carries a briefcase these days? Is this guy for real?* But I did not say that. Instead, I said, "I have my hair all braided up. I'll be wearing a bright orange short-sleeved jumper and some pumps. I'll be driving an old brown Toyota Corolla car. I'll pick you up around 5:30 p.m."

We arrived early at the coffee shop, and soon after, my friends arrived. I introduced Edem to them and we continued to have cordial conversations.

Soon we realized that the time had passed and the singing group was nowhere to be seen. We asked the owner of the coffee shop if they were coming, and she said they just called to apologize for not being able to make it. So my friends went to their vehicles and brought back two guitars. We then had our own live concert. It was an incredible time, and all too soon it was time to leave.

Now I have never been a night owl, and that did not change much throughout my college years. I love to be in bed early, by 10:30 p.m. at the latest, even on a Friday night. I secretly dreaded the fact that I had to take Edem all the way past my home. Then we would have to wait to cross over the Mississippi drawbridge to and from the Westbank. Then I would have to drop him off and wait again before I could head home to my cozy bed. And that was all the way across on the Westbank side of New Orleans.

I lived with my dad at that time. Edem made the drive easy because he spoke all the way until he told me where to pull up and showed me where his apartment was.

I was just about to say goodbye when the unthinkable happened!

He said, "June, thank you for inviting me. I enjoyed the evening."

"That's great!" I answered.

Then he said, "I have been praying to the Lord about meeting my wife. Would you please pray about building a relationship with me?"

I was speechless. I mumbled something and drove away as quickly as I could. I wondered, *After finally meeting me for the first time? No. This was too soon. Who does he think he is?"*

I resolved to not answer Edem's telephone calls. I told my dad that whenever he called to just take a message. This went on for a while until the God of the universe had to intervene Himself.

Another God Moment

It's no secret, the New Orleans lakefront is home to one of the world's largest mixtures of salt and fresh water (Lake Pontchartrain) that is directly connected to the Gulf of Mexico. The lake spans 40 miles long and 30 miles wide. It is lined with outdoor fun: sailing, biking, outdoor restaurants for great eateries . . . you name it. Whenever I wanted some peace and quiet, I would avoid the faster downtown route to my home. I would put my vehicle on cruise control and glide along, sometimes singing praises to my Lord and praying out loud.

My story unfolded.

It was a lovely spring day in 1987, and I was driving along the winding road toward my home. I drove through the scenic view of pink, blue, and yellow azalea bushes sprinkled along the Lake Pontchartrain waterfront. God entered my world. He obviously wanted to take care of some unfinished business with me.

I needed to know what to do about Edem. So I asked aloud, "Lord, I don't know what to do! Who is this Edem guy?" And in the stillness of my being, I heard, *Edem is "special."*

Once again, I was stunned. Then it hit me like a ton of bricks: This is the revelation of God's plan and purpose. It had been a year since I had received God's message at the retreat in Florida. That evening, He told me that I needed to be patient, He had someone "special" for me. I had hidden that message in my heart.

Edem had taken the risk of sharing his love for me and I had rejected him. He had rested his case in God's hand. Now it was my turn to be obedient to the Lord. So I did what was the easiest thing to do: I cried all the way home!

For the rest of that evening, I kept imaging the worst. However, the next morning, I called Edem. When he picked up the phone and heard it was me, he said, "Welcome back, my friend!" His next question was, "When can we get together?" And you know, I would have liked to say that was the end of the story. However, that was the beginning of over 25 years of learning to take risks and resting in God.

My next hurdle was how to backtrack. I had told my father that I did not want to speak with Edem. So the next day, I did my best to explain what had happened to me. I ended my conversation with my father by saying, "And I'll be having dinner with Edem tonight, so please don't wait for me."

Trust and Obey

My dad stood up and declared, "June, you are making a big mistake! There is no way this relationship would last. He is from Africa, you are from Guyana. Where is Edem working anyway?" I told him, "He's still in school. He works part-time and he's going to graduate soon." My dad laughed and said, "You see, my daughter, life is too hard for you to start dating now. You concentrate on graduating from school, find a teaching job, then you could look for a nice Guyanese young man to marry." I replied, "How many Guyanese men do you know who live around here?"

There was just one. He was the professor at Loyola University who was instrumental in my dad landing a job in the maintenance department there. I could not convince my dad otherwise, so that evening, I left for my dinner date with Edem.

I arrived at Edem's apartment promptly at 6:00 p.m. I climbed the stairs to his second-floor apartment. I was nervous and felt like I was intruding at the same time. I wished I had told Edem, "No, let's meet at a coffee shop or something." Of course, neither of us could afford to eat out in those days.

I rehearsed in my mind how I should apologize to Edem about not answering his calls. What should I say? How would he respond? Then I knocked quietly on the wood-framed, cream-colored door. Edem greeted me with a smile and invited me in. I had started to remove my shoes (most Caribbean/ Guyanese and Asian cultures remove their shoes as a sign of acceptance of an invitation that says, "I am comfortable. I feel welcomed and at home!"), but Edem said, "It's okay, go ahead and keep your shoes on." I followed him inside the large open room, separated by living room furniture on the right and a dining room on the left.

"Do you live alone?" I asked.

He said, "No, my roommate left for Guatemala to visit his family. He is married and has children."

The table was set for two, but in the center was a meal fit to feed a large family of eight. I asked if he was expecting some other friends and he said no. He explained that he wanted to surprise me. He learned to cook in Ghana by hanging out with his mother in the kitchen, and when his dad moved to various towns to accept his bank managerial positions, he had a cook. Edem would take cooking lessons from the cook.

The colorful vegetable salad was beautiful. Every piece of lettuce, chopped carrot, sliced cucumber, tomato, and avocado pear was laid out as a work of art. The main courses were jollof rice, stewed chicken, fried plantains, and a light soup served with akple. All of my fears and anxiety disappeared, and we sat down to eat.

After dinner, we sat in the living room to relax. We chatted about how his training and work was going. He was processing data using FORTRAN in his biostatistics course and was excited about doing research. We spoke about his family in Ghana. He shared about his passion to help poor people in the villages around his hometown. I spoke about how I missed my village and my country. He knew of a lady from my village, Buxton, because she was married to one of his cousins who had immigrated to Canada years ago. I shared about my time living in Barbados and how much I loved the whitewashed sand and the blue colored water and the historical parks and sites. My dream was to go back to visit one day.

We bonded over our love for God and how we have always needed to trust Him throughout our lives. We had listened to the same hymns and the same contemporary Christian voices. Our passion to become more like Christ was a shared priority.

We shared about how difficult it had been to be the outlier in each of our church congregations. We were both attending majority White churches.

His apartment was located on the Westbank and mine on the Eastbank of New Orleans. We have always had to dare to be different. But, like me, he was not going to allow America's infatuation with race be his trump card. He, like me, wanted to be first in everything. He wanted to be top of his class. I wanted to also be top of my class, but I was a bit distracted those days. Little did we know the changes that would unfold in our lives together as a couple.

Our biggest decision was whether to remain steady friends or get married right away. One of our greatest limitations was financial resources. We had ourselves, which mattered the most. I was still an undergraduate student at the University of New Orleans. Edem was working as a graduate assistant, earning $8,000 per year at Louisiana State University. He was already a medical doctor in Ghana but wanted to do research in the Biometric Department of LSU. He was enjoying teaching part-time and attending graduate school.

We had no choice; we were between hope and a God place! So we decided to "tie the knot" anyway.

We literally had to depend on God for every need. We prayed for everything. We would call each other on the phone. We made lists of needs and then prayed about each item. Our friends and my church family and my relatives rallied around us and provided all the support we needed. A dear friend of mine called me one day and told me that I needed to rush down to the mall because a jewelry store was going out of business and everything was going on sale. The problem was, we had no disposable cash. I had money in my checking account to pay for my final tuition in order for me to graduate in the summer from the University of New Orleans. I decided to withdraw the funds to buy our wedding bands.

Looking back, it was a risky thing to do. That same friend took me shopping for my wedding dress, shoes, etc., and I was able to purchase everything I needed for under $300! My cousins decided that their wedding gift to us was a stay at a hotel in Mississippi for two nights. My old brown Toyota vehicle was not in good shape to make the trip out of state and back. My best friend loaned us her brand new red Toyota Corolla for our travel to and from our honeymoon.

One Saturday in August 1988, we exchanged our wedding vows at the predominantly White church, Lakeview Christian Center, before one of the most multicultural group of witnesses in America. The reception followed afterward in the church hall. All of my friends rehearsed and played musical instruments in our wedding. Some of my friends even volunteered to decorate the church for our wedding ceremony. The small wedding party was a hodgepodge of family and friends. My dad, dressed in his white tailored suit, stood tall, erect, but sad, and gave me away. A family friend stood in for Edem's father. His parents could not travel from Ghana at the time to attend our wedding. A Ghanaian friend was Edem's best man. My sister Nola was scheduled to be my bridesmaid, but she could not, so my cousin (Dr. Grace Schultz) replaced her. My father's landlord's daughter was my flower girl. My Cousin Melchis was the ring bearer. Edem arranged with Pastor Michael Indest and surprised me by reading a poem ("The Missing Rib") that he had written for me. The poem beautifully depicted the story of God's creation of man in His own image. Then God thought that it was not good for man to be alone, so he created woman.

Edem brilliantly wove the medical imagery of use of modern anesthesia to make him fall into a deep sleep before dislocating one of his ribs from his side to form woman. This woman is now bone of his bone and flesh of his flesh. His rib is missing since he was born. He asked, where was his rib? Most of our guests at the wedding were laughing at that time. Edem felt that the search for his rib was more difficult than digging for and finding gold and diamonds. Only the Creator could help Edem find his rib.

I was shocked by the beautiful poetic imagery on display. Everyone was surprised and loved the poem. People cheered! Years later, I asked him when he was going to write me another poem. He smiled and said, "One of these days."

My African American friend Greg, who had lectured me about attending a predominately White church, could not make it to our wedding. I felt disappointed. I wanted him to see and experience what it was like to have White people demonstrate their love by gifting us their musical talents and skills to make our wedding special. Edem and I could not have afforded to pay them, but they served us with joy!

However, two of Greg's sisters attended the wedding. We had guests from India, Nigeria, Ghana, China, Italy, Cameroon, Guyana, Jamaica, Barbados, Trinidad and Tobago, and the United States of America.

Imagine the potluck-style dinner after we exchanged our wedding vows! The cuisine looked spectacular and tasted delicious. The table was laden with plates and dishes of chicken curry,[48] roti and pourie, meat pies, cheese straws, spinach stew,

---

48. "Guyanese Chicken Curry – Collaboration with Trini Indian Kitchen – Episode 61," YouTube video, 10:17, April 20, 2018, https://www.youtube.com/watch?v=CC7jNGm6B4Y.

and cook-up rice[49] and garbanzo beans. We had lentils served
with mushrooms, cabbage, beans in a savory sauce, garlic
pork,[50] and chicken chow mein.[51] Guests brought a variety of
salads. There were cakes and other desserts and lots to drink
and be merry.

There were many great speeches and well-wishes. A num-
ber of our friends from Louisiana State University Medical
School bowed down to Edem and me (Dr. and Mrs. Edem
Agamah). Everyone laughed!

In the end, all of our friends came on stage to hug us, the
newlyweds, Dr. and Mrs. Edem Agamah. They felt like they
were witnessing a bit of a miracle. In the midst of everything,
God's name was glorified.

Ultimately, this concept of "bringing the world together"
would remain a constant in our union for years to come.

University of New Orleans Graduate School

The University of New Orleans Graduate School was my
next stop after undergraduate studies in my journey. My father and I had shared an apartment, but after I got married, he
moved into a one-bedroom apartment. Meanwhile, my husband's apartment lease was up, so at the time we exchanged
our marriage vows, we did not have a place to stay. Since I had
already been accepted to graduate school, I had applied and

49. "Guyanese Cook-Up Rice," Jehan Can Cook, http://jehancancook.
com/2010/03/a-traditional-guyanese-cook-up-rice/.
50. Guyana Inc. Staff, "Christmas Recipe: Garlic Pork," Guyana Inc., http://
guyanainc.biz/daily-updates/christmas-recipe-garlic-pork/.
51. "Chicken Chow Mein," Jehan Can Cook, http://jehancancook.
com/2019/01/1192/.

was found eligible for an apartment in the University of New
Orleans married student's dorm. The room was not going to
be ready until the week after our return from our honeymoon.

Our friends came to the rescue again. A couple loaned us
the use of their home while they were on summer vacation.
So, when college resumed, we moved into the married student
dorm. We loved it! We were able to save on our rent, water,
and light bill. We created a budget and somehow survived on
Edem's stipend received from Louisiana State University for
teaching graduate students.

We could not eat out or go on dates. We went shopping together, cooked several meals, and stored them in Tupperware
for the rest of the week. We ate dinner together and then returned to LSU for Edem to complete his work and do research
and for me to study.

I took courses in research methodology, developmen-
tal psychology, and public communication. A Chapman
University survey on American fears and anxieties across a
number of topics such as personal safety, the government,
disasters, etc., found that over 25.3 percent of people feared
public speaking in front of large crowds is America.[52]

My most embarrassing experience occurred during my
first public speaking class in school. I had worked hard on
my speech and felt confident that I would do a great job. I
had hoped that because my last name is Wood, the professor
would call me later to do my presentation. I was called sec-

52. Christopher Ingraham, "America's Top Fears: Public Speaking,
Heights and Bugs," *Washington Post,* October 30, 2014, https://
www.washingtonpost.com/news/wonk/wp/2014/10/30/
clowns-are-twice-as-scary-to-democrats-as-they-are-to-republicans/.

ond. The problem was that the nervous sweat appeared on my forehead as soon as my name was called. My palms felt like someone had poured ice-cold water on them. I struggled to walk. On my short walk to the podium, my legs felt like lead, then jelly. The critical scripts assaulted my mind, *You know people can see you are nervous.*

I fumbled through my presentation. I don't remember looking up once as I stumbled my way through it.

However, like they say, "familiarity breeds contempt." After giving many more presentations and participating in discussion groups that semester, I gained confidence. That public communications course was, by far, one of the most important courses that I took in graduate school. Today, I am able to speak confidently in front of large crowds of people.

As a result, my life has never been the same. I have learned how to take risks while trusting in God's permissive will. My faith in God and His provision grew as I trusted Him more and more.

After moving from New Orleans, to Evanston, Illinois, in 1990, we started our family. Our first daughter, Sarah, was born that year. After Edem completed his Internal Medicine residency at St. Francis Hospital, in Evanston, Illinois, we moved to Chicago for him to complete his Fellowship in Oncology/Hematology at the University of Chicago.

10.

Stopover in Chicago

*There is a saying about life not being measured by the
number of breaths you take or the number of heartbeats in
your chest, but by the things that take your breath away.*
—ANONYMOUS

Change is constant. What kinds of changes have you faced as
you began new things in your life?

For us, moving to Chicago came with new sights and
new loves. We lived in Hyde Park, a Chicago subdivision, in
a three-bedroom apartment. We fell in love with the architectural beauty of the buildings and its surroundings. It was
a vintage walk-up with a large open dining room and living
room with hardwood spaces. Our apartment was on the
third floor. It had large windows that allowed for sunlight
and breathtaking views of beautiful gardens and buildings. In
the spring and summer, I could see climbing purple, pink, or
white Confederate jasmine vines through these windows.

For a Guyanese tropical transplant like me, the Chicago
winter snow could be relentless! The view from our third-
floor window was a camouflage of white, fluffy snowcapped

rooftops. The treetops weighed down by the snow were transformed overnight from a soft snowflake covering into heavy
icicles.

There were very few garages in our neighborhood. So in
the mornings after it snowed all night, we would awake to the
scraping sounds of the huge trucks gliding along the main
roads. Our neighbors were chipping ice from windshields. My
husband had to bundle up. He looked like a penguin in thick,
heavy boots and winter hats and gloves in order to make the
mile walk to and from the University of Chicago.

If you have never driven in snow, you may approach it with
the same overconfidence that we did. It is a hard-learned lesson when you figure out how little you can trust the snow-
white beauty.

I recall an incident that occurred in the late 1988/1989
during our first traveling adventures from New Orleans to the
north in search of a residency position for my husband. It was
winter and neither of us had seen and driven in snow before.
We loved the sight of the pristine whiteness of snow on the
side of roads and on rooftops. *So this is what Nat King Cole
sang about,* I mused as I looked outside from the safety of our
car.

We were doing great, or so we thought. We were traveling
along I-55 North in our pint-sized Toyota car when we came
upon a huge 18-wheeler. We felt the power and force of its
engine as it swooshed past us. We were literally blown off the
main road into the ditch! It happened so quickly, all we could
utter was "Jesus! Help!" We were fortunate in that our vehicle
landed on its four wheels. We were terrified! Then, thankful
that we had escaped physical injuries and damage to our vehicle, we sat in our car, praying that a rescue tow truck would

arrive. One did shortly arrive thereafter. It hooked its sturdy tow chains to our front axle and pulled us to safety out of the ditch. We were elated and thanked God for traveling mercies. We continued on our journey to Evanston then to Chicago for the interviews.

In the summer of 1990, we had moved to Evanston. Edem accepted a residency position in Internal Medicine at the St. Francis Hospital in Evanston. Life in Evanston was interesting. I was determined to find work that did not involve teaching. Every weekend, I combed through the employment ad section, circled the prospective ones, and mailed in my applications. I did that while Edem plunged into his new environment. He walked to work so that I could use the car to attend interviews, go shopping, and run errands. I finally landed a telephone operator's job at a store in a suburban mall in the outskirts of Chicago.

Evanston is located in such a way that one has to go around the Chicago North Shore to get to most places. I had never lived in a big city with street numberings such as Chicago's. I had to pass through Chicago to go to the suburbs. I spent most of the first two months getting lost in traffic backed up for miles on end. Most of the time I did not know whether I was going or coming. I could not figure out which were northbound or southbound streets. When I came to exits, I could not decipher which way to go.

After getting lost a number of times, I found out that Chicago streets are laid out according to the grid system. Address numbering begins downtown at State and Madison Street. State Street runs east to west and Madison Street runs north to south. The major streets are about a mile apart and have numbers which are multiples of 800. For example, 87th

Street is 8700 south.[53] Once I figured the north- to southbound and the west- to eastbound streets, driving to places became more manageable.

I became the driving guru in our household since my husband spent most of his time at work then walked home. We would consult our map trip maker each time we needed to go somewhere.

Our friends invited us to their church in Winnetka, Illinois. So, every Sunday morning, we headed up further north west to attend church. We were still attending Winnetka Bible Church when I got pregnant. So my first daughter, Sarah, was the only child of color in the nursery. As a matter of fact, we represented the small number (0.1 percent) of Black families in that part of the country. We attended Winnetka Bible Church until we moved to Chicago. Once in Chicago, we attended the Moody Bible Church by the Chicago Lakefront.

Prior to our arrival, in 1979–1984, Hyde Park was designated a state Historic District. The Hyde Park-Kenwood area between East 47th and East 59th streets, South Grove Avenue, and the lake became our stomping ground for the next two years. Our apartment, off Greenwood Ave., was right across from one of the many local parks. It was conveniently located within walking distance of the iconic University of Chicago. We owned a small Toyota car, but my husband walked to and from the university each day. I used the car to go to work at a

---

53. "Chicago's Street Numbering System," Chicago Rail Fan, https://www.chicagorailfan.com/streetno.html#:~:text=Chicago%20address%20numbering%20begins%20downtown,east%2Dwest%20streets%20are%20numbered.

building across from the Illinois Masonic Medical Center in Chicago.

As new parents, we searched to find someone who would be able to take care of Sarah. We found a wonderful babysitter for her. Annie was a short, petite Trinidadian lady with beautiful olive skin, green eyes, and a beautiful smile. She spoke with a sing-song Trinidadian accent. She spoke in the kind of tone that made you smile: "All you comin over soon? Yu kno' I'm always here, man." She had two beautiful daughters; one daughter was Sarah's age, and the other was five years older. The two younger girls connected immediately! When the older sister went off to grade school, they would spend most of their time jumping, chasing each other around, and having the time of their lives. This, of course, helped Annie to work around her home freely without having to entertain her daughter.

In the mornings, I dropped Sarah off at Anne's house. Then I continued driving the 14 miles to work in Chicago. After work, I headed back to Annie's to pick up Sarah. I was thrilled to see how happy she was to see me. Then we drove home to prepare dinner.

I was working for Aurora University, a private liberal arts college located in Aurora, Illinois. In the 1970s and 1980s, the university wanted to expand its curriculum outside of the Aurora area to Wisconsin, the Lake Geneva area, and Chicago. They partnered with the Illinois Masonic Medical Center in Chicago to provide undergraduate and graduate education in nursing. Nursing students in the Chicago metropolitan areas benefited because they did not have to commute all the way to Aurora to obtain their nursing degrees. This was a perfect match. Students had access to the hospital's resources to complete their RN, BSN, and master's level nursing degree through Aurora University.

As assistant to the dean of student services, part of my responsibility was to travel to the Aurora University campus twice monthly to attend meetings. I also did local outreach/recruitment to junior colleges and universities in the Chicago area on behalf of the university.

I had to maintain regular office hours in my office in Chicago, located across the street from the hospital. Students had ready access to me to assist them with planning and executing their academic progress throughout their time at the school. Students would apply for admission to Aurora University's RN and bachelor programs, and my role was to determine if they were eligible to apply for the nursing program, give clear understanding of what was expected of them once they were accepted, and map out a plan to graduate students in a timely manner. Apart from one secretary and a part-time office assistant and myself, there were no other employees at the site. We were the face of Aurora University. So I spent most of my days at work, interacting with potential and current nursing students.

Many moments of our lives will create not only a big impact but also a memorable impression. I remember one disturbing incident that occurred during one of the busy fall registration seasons. I was busy interviewing, registering, and answering student inquiries on the phone. That day, I was so busy that I did not have time to go on lunch break. I decided to work throughout so that I could attend to the growing number of students waiting in line to see me.

When it was time for me to leave to go home, I could not find my purse! I had one special place in my desk drawer where I always placed my purse. I soon realized that some-one had stolen my purse. I quickly called the Illinois Masonic Medical Center Police Department, and they immediately came over to my office. They looked everywhere, but they could not find my purse. They took all my pertinent infor-mation and we looked at the list of names of students whom I came into contact with that day. I finally locked my office and headed home for the night.

The next morning, I received a call from the police. They had continued looking for my purse and found it thrown in the bushes behind my office. Whoever stole my purse was looking for money, because all my important cards were in-tact and only the money was stolen. I breathed a sigh of relief! I had already called to cancel the credit card that was in my purse and was dreading having to apply for new driver's li-cense, etc. We never did catch the culprit who stole my purse.

Apart from that incident, I enjoyed working with adults more than I did teaching children in a classroom setting. I was settling in nicely in that position as the assistant to the dean of student services.

I remember the day I discovered that I was pregnant with our middle daughter, Aseye, as if it were yesterday. The news of my pregnancy did not sit well with me. I had worked out a plan to go running on the University of Chicago's campus track in Hyde Park twice a week. My goal was to get back in shape quickly. This news was a bend in the road. I had to wres-tle with the reality that I might not lose weight as planned. However, I continued working out in moderation up until it was no longer safe to do so.

Meanwhile, Edem's increased responsibilities as a Hematology Oncology Fellow at the University of Chicago were becoming unbearable! He was on call every weekend and was constantly tired and exhausted. We were both finding it difficult to keep up with the work responsibilities and raising our young family. He was gone for extended periods of time. I attended most of my well-baby care appointments alone. I often felt lonely, frustrated, and tired. I continued to work up to the eighth month of my pregnancy.

My husband and I took careful and objective evaluation of our family life and decided that it was best for me to stay at home and raise our two children. I resigned from my position in 1993. Later that year, our middle daughter was born. Then, to make matters worse, I got pregnant again within 17 months! In April 1995, our third daughter was born. I remember shedding tears, because I felt like I was going to be pregnant for the rest of my life! My husband reassured me that everything was by God's design. If we had not gotten pregnant then and had the baby before leaving the University of Chicago, it would have been difficult for us to afford insurance coverage for delivering a baby during the transition period between jobs. And, once again, my husband was right. We later received a call from one of his physician friends, who had changed jobs and moved while his wife was pregnant. The cost of delivery of their son without insurance coverage was exorbitant!

Then, to make matters worse, the washer and dryer were located in the basement of the apartment building. With one child, things were bearable. So imagine having to cart all three children up and down three flights of stairs every time I did the laundry. Going to the park was not easy either. We had to be extremely careful climbing up the steep stairways and getting down. I tried to take the children as often as I could to the

Museum of Science and Industry or to the Shedd Aquarium, located in walking and wheeling distances from our apartment.

We spent hours at the local parks, observing and enjoying the beautiful blooms and colorful vegetation around the Hyde Park neighborhood. Sometimes we met other mothers with young children. We listened to what was then foreign to my children, like the twitter of the hummingbird searching for food. I had the children lie on their backs and look up into the sky.

"See the clouds?" I'd ask my two older children.

We'd watch as the clouds rippled, spread out, and folded over as the sun cast its golden glow underneath to form ridges of yellow, blue, and orange. Sometimes, we saw sinister clouds glowing in the west and the whole sky alive with clouds of ever-changing shapes and contour. Conversations were easy then. No words were necessary. Just the quietness of nature turning around on its head right before our eyes. Then, during the winter, I would bundle the children, gather their sleds, cross the street in the local park, and let them careen down the side of the hill. It was a lot of work cleaning up afterward, but it was all worth it!

In retrospect, life was not all that bad. On three occasions, I had some help with the children. My father- and mother-in-law came to assist us. Since my dad had retired from Loyola University by then, he and my in-laws took turns assisting me during the day, during their visits to see the grandchildren. Two months after our youngest child was born in 1995, our family of five moved to Springfield, Illinois.

Becoming Bobby

For a gentleman in his late 60s, my father was a tall, slightly built man, with large, rough hands that could lift timber and boulders over his frame with ease. He moved about with an air of authority and carried an encyclopedia in his brain. He knew the days, months, and years of his relatives' birthdays, marriage, or when they died, etc. He could calculate large amounts of numbers in his head.

I do not remember when or how the changes in my father occurred. All I know is that I witnessed a transformation in his attitude toward life. Like the blowing of the wind, I cannot put a date or a period as to when this metamorphosis occurred. All I know is that after our first daughter was born, my father returned from Guyana to the United States to visit us in Evanston. He arrived when she was just beginning to formulate words.

A few days after his arrival, my daughter was being fussy. I heard my father say, "Caryl, bring her to me, she feeling sleepy. I'll rock her to sleep."

I was taken aback by his request. I could not recall seeing my dad holding a child before. I carefully slid my precious bundle into his lap. I watched as he tenderly held his grandchild in his rough hands and rocked her softly until she fell asleep. Later, my dad said, "I used to rock you like dat when you were little, you know?"

That summer, with outstretched arms toward him, I heard my daughter's utterance, "Bobby! Bobby!" She wanted to be carried in those strong arms of her grandfather's. And that's how my father was crowned "Bobby" for the rest of his life in the Agamah household.

Over the years, as our children grew older, Bobby would return to America from Guyana to watch his grandchildren participate in ballgames. He attended their music recitals and birthdays and their graduation ceremonies from high school and college. He remained, *Bobby*!

Over the years, we discovered that my father loved poetry and he could quote long speeches and wise sayings. To the delight of our three children, Bobby would regularly perform for them, in a funny and hilarious manner. He memorized lengthy poems and songs. His favorite poem was "The Brook" by Alfred Lord Tennyson. There is a refrain in the poem, "For men may come and men may go, But I go on forever!"[54] My girls would imitate Bobby's baritone inflection and squeal with delight.

My father loved big words. He named his children lengthy British names as Shakespeare, Rudolph, Dana, and Ingrid, and he named me June Caryl. Whenever my dad was in a good mood, he would enunciate each name with such grace and pride in his British/Guyanese drawl. He seemed to have defied all logic that in order to be "successful," one needed to have obtained a high school or college degree.

When my father was in his late 80s, he reluctantly moved in with our family. He lived in our home until he lost his battle with Alzheimer's disease. In January 2011, we flew his body to Guyana, and his remains were buried next to his mother's grave.

---

54. Alfred Lord Tennyson, "The Brook Summary and Analysis," LitCharts, https://www.litcharts.com/poetry/alfred-lord-tennyson/the-brook.

Questions for General Reflection
or Group Discussion
(Use the space below to respond)

1. How has your own life experience clouded or enhanced your ability to see value in learning about others that are different from you?

2. What events in your life has been the hardest to accept and surrender to God's will?

3. As you reflect on some theme (example, Hard work, Sacrifice, Adventure, Acceptance, Risk) in my story, which of those are dominant in yours?

11.

Life in Springfield, Illinois

*My mission in life is not merely to survive, but to thrive;
and to do so with passion, some compassion, some humor,
and some style. I'll try to be a rainbow in someone's cloud.*
—MAYA ANGELOU

The Minority Family

There will be times when you just don't fit in. That was something we had grown used to.

We arrived in Springfield, Illinois, in the summer of 1995. Prior to my husband's decision to join the Central Illinois Hematology Oncology Center (CIHOC), he had spent months interviewing with prospective oncology private practices while I was pregnant with our third daughter, Miriam.

During our last visit to Springfield, we looked at homes in several neighborhoods. Our current home was one of the last ones that we considered purchasing. I had rolled my pregnant frame out of our car, it seemed for the tenth time, and felt the sharp pain shoot down from somewhere on my right side, down to my middle toe! This too reminded me of the foreign sound of the heartbeat of another human being emanating from my tummy, the first time I had an ultrasound. What a great welcome home!

Now, baby number three was two months old, and we were beginning a new phase in my journey. Our 40 feet of moving van was late on arrival. So, the first night, all five of us snuggled under blankets on a king-size mattress on the floor in the master bedroom. We had no window curtains to shield us from the prying eyes of the outside world. We managed somehow until our stuff arrived.

The next day, we heard a knock on our front door, and it was one of our next-door neighbors, Mrs. Cynthia Shambley. She wanted to welcome us to the neighborhood. She gave us her telephone number and told us to call anytime we needed assistance with anything. For the next two weeks, she faithfully came over, answered my questions, and showed me how to lock and unlock some of our doors. She was a teacher and listened patiently to our fears and concerns. Her family of four were some of the first people of color to move into this subdivision, and she vowed that the neighbors were very friendly and caring. She gave us tips about the best places to shop for groceries, curtains, and other household items. We felt welcomed in our new environment.

College in Springfield

Whenever my husband interviewed in search of a job, I would say, "Find out whether they have a university in that city, I want to attend graduate school." Since I had started graduate school in New Orleans, I wanted to complete some kind of degree as soon as possible. I recall one time my husband asked me, "Do you want this degree just so you get a degree, or do you want a degree that would enable you to get a career?" I was a bit offended, but I later realized that he was being practical. Who was going to take care of our precious ones when he is busy starting a private medical practice and I was working full time? I told him, "I need to finish graduate school soon." And I did!

I applied for admission to attend graduate school at the University of Illinois in Springfield. I could only attend at night. My husband worked all day and three nights per week, but he watched the children so that I could attend classes. This arrangement was life-giving to me. I had the opportunity to engage in adult conversation and I found the rigors of academia very stimulating.

Ever since I lost my mom, the question of access to quality health care and who and what determines that access plagued me. So from the first night of classes, I think I fell in love with studying the concept and principles governing public health. I learned about the social determinants of health: access to adequate housing, transportation, access to care (physical and mental), quality education (from kindergarten to college), and how these play a role in people's quality of education, life, and longevity. I was hooked! I was always fascinated because I had finally come to the realization that because trusted resources are few and expensive, a large percentage of the American population, if poor, will suffer great loss.

As public health practitioners, we studied cases and came to the realization that the means to address mental and physical health should be a precursor to improving the systems that impact all the above social determinants of health. Public health touches every aspect of our existence in life. It affects the quality of foods we eat. It seeks to address the safety and quality of the milk and water we drink. We studied about "food deserts" in this, one of the richest countries in the world!

Food deserts are areas where people experience food insecurity.[55] We all know what it feels like when we have not eaten all day. But can we measure how hungry we are? When, as a child, I hated metemgee and had to go without a meal, was that food insecurity? Hunger is a feeling, but food insecurity lets us measure the conditions which can lead to hunger.

In public health we look at people's tendency to have to choose between buying food or medicine. We study behaviors of people who are underemployed or unemployed in regard to access to food while in poor health and its effect on children and the adults themselves. In America, over 40 million people depend on food banks at some point in their lives to survive.[56]

I chose public heath because I enjoy learning about how to go about improving the global health of people around the world. After four years, I earned a master of public health (MPH) degree in 2001 from the University of Illinois at Springfield.

When the university celebrated its 50th anniversary in 2020, I was thrilled to learn I was among several alumni featured in a university newsletter commemorating the university's history and student achievements. What an honor and a

55. "How Do You Measure Hunger?" Feeding America, https://www.feedingamerica.org/hunger-in-america/food-insecurity.
56. "11 Facts about Hunger in the US," Do Something, https://www.dosomething.org/us/facts/11-facts-about-hunger-us#:~:text=In%202017%2C%2040%20million%20people,million%20households%20were%20food%20insecure.

blessing to be recognized among such a prestigious group of graduates!

* * *

You really have to look inside yourself and
find yourself and find your own inner strength,
and say, "I'm just going to be myself."
—MARIAH CAREY

Finding Church, School, and Friends

During the search for our home, we passed by the Hope Church building. Once we decided to purchase our home, I said to my husband, "Honey, we need to find a church in this neighborhood." My husband responded, "That's the church we are going to attend," as he pointed in the direction of the Hope Church on the corner. "But we haven't visited any church yet," I complained.

Despite not having a place as we were beginning that search, my husband was right again. We hauled our three children every Sunday morning and attended this predominantly White church about 10 minutes away from our home. We, the Agamah family, planted ourselves there. And because my husband and I are both creatures of habit, we never left that church.

Over the years we have seen friends of ours leave the church for a number of reasons. Some left and came back, but we, the Agamahs, have stayed the course. We became the face of the outliers; non-White individuals in the predominantly White Hope Church community for the longest time.

However, over recent years there has been an influx of international professional minority groups in Springfield. The medical community and Hope Church have benefited from their immigration to Springfield by creating more diversity in the three major medical institutions and other state government facilities.

My youngest daughter, Miriam, also gained a reputation and went on record as the loudest crying baby ever to stay in the Hope Church nursery. Most Sunday mornings, when I took her to the nursery, she would be asleep. Once the helpers took her out of her chair and laid her in the nursery crib, she would sleep for half an hour. When she awoke, her thunderous screams would awake the rest of the sleeping newborns and toddlers. It would be pandemonium in that small nursery until I recognized the emergency blinking of the tiny number on the top right of the church sanctuary wall. I had to hustle to rescue her. She would sob in my arms until she felt comforted. Little Miriam hated going to the nursery on Sundays!

Miriam continued to cling to me (her mama). It was difficult for me to go most places without Miriam. Most days, I could not keep up with the responsibilities of three young ones, and by the end of the day, I was very exhausted. I desperately needed a playmate for her. Later, I was listening to a program about child development and learned that what Miriam needed was a form of secure attachment with me. Once that bond is secure, this would allow her to slowly feel safe with others. I needed to be patient with her. I was thankful that I could be home with her throughout the day. I regularly took her in my arms, looked her in the eyes, spoke to her softly, and hugged her tightly.

One day, I called my friend Tammy. She worked in the nursery at church and always seemed to do well with the babies. I asked her if Miriam and I could come by and spend some time with her and her preschooler in her home. We visited for a month until Miriam got used to playing with her daughter. Then, one day, we did an experiment. I left quietly while the toddlers were playing. From that day forward, my Miriam was able to stay with my "baby whisperer" friend Tammy. That experience taught me a number of lessons. First, each child is different, and they have individual needs. Second, it is okay to ask for help even when you feel doubtful or unsure, and third, mothers are the best encouragers!

When our children grew older, they insisted on remaining in the main church for Sunday services. We tried encouraging them to attend Sunday school with their age group, but they insisted on worshipping with us each Sunday. Since some other families' children did the same, we thought nothing of their choice. They claimed at the time that they enjoyed staying in "big" church. Later, I learned the real reasons for their reluctance to join their peers.

As the only Black children in the youth service, our children did not feel welcomed, as no one connected with them. It was always one-sided. They were the ones who had to attempt to reach out to their peers. As they matured, went away to college, and returned to Springfield, they joined young adult groups and felt more comfortable being amongst their church peers. They even volunteered in the nursery and took on leadership and service roles in areas of personal interest.

Finding the right school for our oldest daughter was fore-
most on our minds. We only had one vehicle at that time, so
my husband used it to go work and back. I listened to a number of programs on the radio about homeschooling, and I felt
comfortable about teaching my two preschoolers at home. So,
mostly out of convenience, I decided to homeschool our two
older children. Then, when our oldest was ready for kindergarten, we enrolled her in a private Christian school. We still
only owned one vehicle, but we made it work somehow.

I began to make more friends as I took the children for
walks in the neighborhood. We then discovered that apart
from our neighbor that came over to assist us the day of our
arrival, we were the only other family of color in the whole
neighborhood! There were a few other Black families in other
subdivisions, including a Ghanaian family of five. How can we
raise our little Brown girls in this environment? We desperately searched for other Black and Brown kids at the private
elementary school but found very few children of color.

Then, in 2000, we received one of the best gifts ever. These
gifts came in small packages that did not look like us in the
form of the Kirby family. Their two boys, Ryan and Josh, were
the exact same ages as our girls. The Agamah girls and the
Kirby boys were the only young children on our block. For
years, they had a great time creating childhood memories!
Our kids connected immediately and so did their parents with
Edem and me.

Summer of 2000 was a pivotal time in tennis history. The
Williams sisters, Venus and Serena, became the faces of tennis for all Black girls and women of color. Venus won her
first Wimbledon title against defending champion Lindsey
Davenport in July 2000. She became the second African

American woman after Althea Gibson won back-to-back Wimbledon titles in 1957 and 1978.[57] Over the years, our family could not get enough of watching and reading about their many exploits. Our girls, Aseye and Miriam, pretended to be Venus and Serena and the Kirby boys, Ryan and Joshua, morphed into Andre Agassi and Roger Federer. They played doubles tennis for hours on both the Agamah's and Kirby's driveways. Years later, the Agamah girls went on to play tennis throughout their high school years. The Lord had answered our prayers in His own way and in His own time in bringing the Kirbys across the street.

At the time of our arrival in 1995, the medical community in Springfield had three major hospitals. To our amazement, unlike Chicago, where our children's pediatrician was a beautiful woman of color, there were none in Springfield. We had left Hyde Park, which housed a rainbow of beautiful shades of people representing all nations of the world. We were to learn the difficult art of transcending and yet owning our identity as minorities.

We discovered that among those three medical institutions, there were only a handful of Black physicians and professionals working in them. Everywhere I took the girls, the people who waited on us were White. Whether we went to the bank, the doctor's office, the grocery store, or the post office, we were surrounded by White faces and spaces.

---

57. "Venus Williams Wins Wimbledon for the First Time," July 10, 2019, *History*.com, https://www.history.com/this-day-in-history/venus-williams-wins-wimbledon.

Before moving to Springfield, we were told that Springfield is the Land of Lincoln. Surely there would be a higher representation of people of color in this city. It would take us living in Springfield for over 15 years before we learned part of the reason why Springfield, the great Land of Lincoln, was the way it is now.

* * *

The stone which cannot be lifted should be kissed.
—An Arabic Proverb

Soccer Mom

After I graduated from the University of Illinois, I realized that most of what I had studied in public health classes could be used on the ground in Ghana. In 1996, the International Health and Development Network (IHDN), a medical mission nonprofit organization, was formed to develop effective and sustainable primary health care programs in small towns and villages in the developing world. IHDN uses the earthly work of Jesus Christ as a model. There were tremendous needs in Ghana. I became the logistics coordinator for the IHDN Mission and volunteered my services, while working from home, in Springfield.

My husband's workload in his practice as a hematologist/ oncologist in Springfield had increased. Instead of finding employment in the Department of Public Health there, I made the choice to become the often lone, dark face of a suburban "soccer mom."

We had folded neatly into the token few-and-in-between Black family slot in the cornfields of Springfield. We had started our family life in the well-heeled northern suburb of Evanston. Then we moved into upscale Hyde Park in Chicago, not too far from where the first African American president of America, Barak Obama (and his family), resided. We did not think much about how our children would fare in this environment.

We soon became comfortable with suburban life, our family—as more often than not—the only family of color with children in the soccer, basketball, and volleyball home and away games. I would volunteer to be the driver for most away games when our children were in grade school. When our children participated in music and choir competitions out of town, I drove.

During elementary and high school track and field events, my van became the favorite to drive in. I made sure I refilled the goodie bins with healthy snacks and had the ice-chest filled with cold water for the trips. Then, when all three of the Agamah girls did track and field, volleyball, and tennis, I was willing and able to be the extra driver. Most of my children's friends preferred to ride in my van. I would eavesdrop on conversations. When the girls needed my opinion on any subject, I was ready to give thoughtful responses to their questions.

People would often ask me what I did for a living. I often debated with myself, *Should I return to work outside of the home? I imagined how wonderful life would be, getting dressed up for work and meeting all those wonderful people and helping them make important decisions about their future.*

At first, I struggled to articulate the important work I was doing, raising minority girls in a suburban world. Then, one day, I came across the term "domestic engineer." I loved the sound of that. It described what I did every day.

My investment in the well-being of my young family meant a great deal to me. I was blessed to be able to afford to be a stay-at-home domestic engineer. I embraced the value of being there for our children's first steps, first words, etc. I later discovered that, partly because I did not have any childhood photos of myself, I went overboard with capturing the moments on film. It got so bad that my children ran away or hid their faces whenever they suspected that I was about to take "another" picture with my camera. Later, as adults, they were grateful to have those cherished mementos of their childhood.

Edem worked long hours to build up his new private practice. Often, I fed the girls early and waited for his arrival before I ate dinner with him. As the girls grew older, they too wanted to stay awake to see their daddy and have him play "Wake up Dragon" with them.

Initially, we did not have any furniture in the formal living room space. This area became the scene for Wake Up, Dragon. Edem would cover his eyes, and the children would hide. He would find them then carry them on his back and shoulders. He pretended that their weight had become unbearable. He would pretend to pass out. Our girls would chant in unison, "Wake up, Dragon! Wake up, Dragon!" "Wake up, Dragon!" The dragon would come to life—slowly, slowly, *very* slowly— then Edem's huge frame would bound up and they would run helter-skelter!! After their baths, we would pray with them and tuck them into bed.

When the girls were old enough to attend elementary school, I tried working part-time but most of those jobs were aborted for a number of reasons. I made a personal decision to work from home because my husband and my children needed me. I especially had to help my children navigate their world during those formative years. I finally resigned myself to using my leadership and organizational skills to volunteer in a number of local nonprofit organizations and was privileged to be founder of some. Over the years I have met, partnered with, and grown to love many of these talented and wonderful doctors' spouses. We share a passion to help the needy in our community.

Landscaping/Gardening

I poured myself into working around our home. While my husband went to work and the children were in school, I occupied my time doing productive chores around our home.

My first job was to create a vegetable garden. Memories of my father's vegetable garden remained intact. I yearned to reproduce a large garden like his, but our yard space was not adequate enough. I had to contend with an aboveground garden that has produced some beautiful, tasty, and satiating vegetables over the years.

Since our subdivision was a fairly new one at the time, I would observe how the landscaping service people planted my neighbor's shrubs and do their landscaping. Then I would hurry over to our local Lowe's for supplies. I packed them in the back of my van. Then I'd dash over to the gardening section of the store. There, I would inquire about which shrubs, bushes, and plants were appropriate to do my landscaping by myself. Once, after planting my shrubs, I ordered some gravel to spread around the yard. The truck dumped it on my driveway. I borrowed my neighbor's wheelbarrow and proceeded to spread gravel around the yard.

That night, as I sat in my family room to relax, I could not get up without feeling a sharp pain in my lower back. I ended up on the floor. I had always prided myself on being a tough lady. I played ping-pong with intensity, and later, after I moved to Springfield and joined the Racquet Club, I played tennis with great passion! Rarely did I complain of aches and pains. So I was shocked by the severity and amount of pain that I was experiencing then.

"What happened to you, honey?" my husband asked me.

"I . . . I . . . don't know," I groaned as I writhed on the floor in agony.

"What did you do today?" he probed.

Then, it suddenly occurred to me that I had strained the muscles in my lower back. In my excitement to do my own landscaping, I did not consider the fact that I had never used a wheelbarrow during the past decade of my life! I had no business doing so then. It took me years to recover from that injury, but I finally did. I learned the African proverb the hard way, "If you want to go fast, go alone. If you want to go far, go together."

* * *

Life is a melting pot of knowledge and experience, both your own and that of everyone around you. Don't be afraid to learn from others mistakes and take bits of useful information or ideas that help you get better at what you do. Wisdom is there at your fingertips, use it.
—DENZEL WASHINGTON

Tennis Lessons

It was a very sad period for another reason. I loved playing tennis. After my injury, I could not play tennis for months. Tennis is a racquet sport. It can be played individually against another individual or two people could play against two others, which is termed "doubles." Each person plays with a racquet that has strings woven across each other within a graphite frame, used to hit yellow felt balls across a net. Players play sets. The first player(s) to win six games with a margin of two games wins the first set. A tennis match could last for as little as one and a half hours to four or five hours.

Tennis is played by millions of people all around the world, but there are four important grand slams played each year. Anyone that visits the Agamah family household is familiar with hearing the characteristic grunting sounds of tennis emanating from our television set in our family room. Throughout the year, the television screen color changes but not the ascending intensity of yelling and shrieking that punctuates the hitting of the tennis ball and the grunting release of air: *Uh, aha, uh, aaah!*

Toward the end of January to the beginning of February, the Australian Open is held in Melbourne Park before packed stands of people around sky-blue hard tennis courts. Then follows the French Open, held in late May, on red rusted-dirt clay courts in Roland Garros, in Paris, France. I marvel at the appearance as players, dressed in clean-cut outfits, grunt and slash their way across the surface with a glide and acrobatic slides to retrieve yellow tennis balls. The sea of white fedora hats, worn by spectators, moving left to right in unison as the players trade cross-court and down-the-line shots. At the end of the games, the colors of their socks are usually unrecogniz-able. Sweat drains from their bodies like a waterfall.

This tournament is then followed by the beautiful, pristine Wimbledon Championships played on grass in England. Most players are required to wear white, and the contrast between the green grass and yellow ball as it skids across the lawn at breathtaking speeds of 100 or more miles per hour is a marvel to watch.

Then the finale of tennis tournaments, the US Open, is played, like the Australian Open, on a hard court in New York at Arthur Ashe Stadium from late August to the first half of September.

I think our family's passion for tennis originated with my love of playing ping-pong. Years ago, I represented my high school at several ping-pong tournaments in Guyana. When I moved to New Orleans, my friend Carol introduced me to tennis. I was hooked! I played throughout my college years at the University of New Orleans. Then, when I met Edem, I was pleasantly surprised to learn that he played tennis when he was at the University of Ghana. He and I played tennis regu-larly when we were first married, but as our family grew and our work schedules changed, it was difficult to answer calls while Edem was on the tennis courts.

My friend Valerie and I had joined the local Racquet Club and really loved the sport. She and I were most often the only two women of color on the courts. When our children were in grade school, we started taking them to the local park to learn and take tennis drills at Washington Park.

One Saturday morning, I invited another friend and her children to join us at Rotary Park to play tennis. The children had teamed up and started hitting the ball around. Ten minutes into this adventure, I heard the high-pitched wailing from my middle daughter as she cowered on the ground. She was holding her lips, and blood was spewing all over the tennis court. Instinctively, I rushed to her assistance and my friend ran to her van to get some ice. Minutes later, I was on the phone, calling my husband with the bad news. Fortunately, he was on call that weekend and told us where we needed to go.

We arrived at the emergency room and soon she was attended to. Then I made a terrible mistake. The attending physician asked, "Ms. Agamah, would you like to come in the room with your daughter? This should not take took long."

Before my brain could catch up with my heart and emotions, I said, "Sure!"

I sat next to the head of the bed where my daughter lay. As soon as the doctor placed the needle next to the wound on Aseye's bottom lip, I was out like a light switch! The next thing I heard was, "Ms. Agamah are you okay?"

I had passed out.

"Here is some orange juice."

I drank the glass of orange juice and I felt much better. I realized then that I had operated on an adrenaline rush. The sight of blood does things to my brain, my muscles, and my breathing. Everything in me wanted to escape! My daughter was in pain, so I felt her pain. And to this day, I cannot look at a needle entering my body or anyone else's without squirming. How can this be when I'm married to a medical doctor and my three children are tough as nails when it comes to dealing with blood and gore?

The Black Table

In his book *Born a Crime: Stories from a South African Childhood,* Trevor Noah said, "But the real world doesn't go away. Racism exists. People are getting hurt. And just because it's not happening to you, doesn't mean it's not happening. And at some point you have to choose; black or white, pick a side. You can try to hide from it. You can say, oh, I don't take a side, but at some point, life will force you to pick a side."[58]

As immigrant parents, we knew nothing about societal biases.[59] Both Edem and I went to high school in Ghana and Guyana. I went to undergraduate and graduate institutions of learning in America. My husband went to graduate and medical schools in this country. We had not developed the muscle to navigate such minefields. According to a Russian proverb, "There is no shame in not knowing; the shame lies in not finding out."

My oldest daughter was about to enter third grade. She brought home a letter from school. The letter asked us whether we wanted our daughter to be in the gifted English and math classes or remain in the regular stream of those courses. Our daughter was a straight A student, so that was music to our ears! She was the only Black student in her class. I signed

---

58. "Trevor Noah > Quotes > Quotable Quotes," from *Born a Crime: Stories from a South African Childhood* (New York: Random House, 2019), Goodreads, https://www.goodreads.com/quotes/8067475-but-the-real-world-doesn-t-go-away-racism-exists-people#:~:text=Racism%20exists.,t%20mean%20it's%20not%20happening.

59. Christopher Haggarty-Weir, "Cognitive Biases and 'Doing Your Own Research,' Part 2 – The Social Biases," March 9, 2013, Mostly Science, https://mostlyscience.com/2013/03/doing-your-own-research-cognitive-biases-and-you-part-2-social-biases/.

the letter in the affirmative and gave it to her to return to her teacher.

When the final list of students was chosen, our daughter's name was not on the list. I made an appointment to see the headmistress of the school. I took along our daughter's stellar report card as evidence to show that she belonged in that track. The headmistress agreed with me, and Sarah was allowed to take those classes. We never received an explanation for why our daughter was not put in the gifted track. However, I am glad we were able to catch the oversight in good time.

All three of my children attended that school from kindergarten to junior high school and received a stellar education. They were accepted and embraced by their teachers and fellow students.

My children thrived in that environment where they learned that they were created in the image of the imago Dei (Latin for "the image of God"). My children learned that there is no limit to their aspiring to become moral, spiritual, and intellectual beings who are loved unconditionally by God. Thurgood Marshall, the first African American US Supreme Court member, said, "In recognizing the humanity of our fellow beings, we pay ourselves the highest tribute."[60]

We were less practiced in Black spaces, since most of our daily existence was in predominantly suburban areas.[61]

---

60. "Quotes," Thurgood Marshall, from *Furman v. Georgia* (1972), Shmoop, https://www.shmoop.com/quotes/in-recognizing-humanity-we-pay-our-selves-the-highest-tribute.html.
61. Allison Martin, "How to Thrive in Predominantly White Spaces as a Minority Trainee," August 20, 2018, Op-Med, https://opmed.doximity.com/articles/how-to-thrive-in-predominantly-white-spaces-as-a-minority-trainee?_csrf_attempted=yes.

The good thing was that we took our kids to their dad's homeland in Ghana every summer, since our youngest daughter was 11 months old. While their friends went to Hawaii and other fun vacation spots, our little girls were packing suitcases for the trip to Ghana, where they learned how to be Black!

While my girls were in high school, I volunteered to work the PTA snack table, located in a corner of the lunchroom. This was the place for students who received small token awards for good behavior during high school classes. I would set up my tubs of goodies and students would exchange their token for candies, cookies, or school supplies.

It was during my stint that I learned that all across America, high schools have what is called the "Black Table." I learned that a majority of White classrooms rarely foster a true belonging for Black children. Black children feel like they must perform, entertain, or tell jokes to be noticed or else suffer the dreaded invisibility that comes with the territory. That is why the Black Table is sacred in high schools.

At the Black Table, minorities become insiders. There is no code-switching. No inside voices and no one there to remind them of the White world's decorum. The Black Table is where they feel safe in their skin. They could be themselves in their group's cocoon. They sat there to feel less alienated. My husband and I were so focused on our own survival that we had no awareness of how our children were navigating their world.

One day, Miriam came home from Washington Park. She and her girlfriend were preparing for an upcoming tennis tournament. Their game was interrupted when they heard the sound of giggling. They saw two or three White boys in the bushes. The boys started yelling at the girls and throwing things onto the tennis court. The boys continued shouting at the girls.

"You two suck because you are Black and we are White!" they yelled. The girls ignored them, and the boys finally went away.

Miriam handled this incident as she handled many others. She blocked the negative things out of her mind and moved on. After that incident, Miriam learned a lesson about what racism looked like. The boys were identifying the basic tenets of racism, such as bigotry, stereotyping, and domination. The boys probably felt that the girls had no business playing tennis, since tennis for the longest time was considered a "White" sport.

Suffice it to say, over the years, I had to discover new language and new words coined by social scientists to describe how minorities survive in American culture.[62] I recently learned about code-switching from my daughter Miriam. This is a term used to describe how minorities try to fit into the corporate world. It is how they survive in these environments.

I asked my daughters if they ever needed to code-switch. One of them said, "I find myself needing to smile more often and change my way of communicating when I have to be in predominately White spaces. It's something we find ourselves doing. Like a muscle that you flex or turn on and off."

"Honey, you love interacting with people. You are warm and engaging. Just be yourself," I said, trying to console her.

---

62. Ida Harris, "Code-Switching Is Not Trying to Fit in to White Culture, It's Surviving It," December 17, 2019, Yes!, https://www.yesmagazine.org/opinion/2019/12/17/culture-code-switching/.

"I know, Mom."

Miriam explained that since college, she has actually mastered the art of code-switching. In a December 17, 2019, *Solutions Journalism* article, Ida Harris describes what happens to the tone of her voice as she introduces herself to a classroom of predominantly White students. Without thought, she shifts her demeanor and speech from a naturally raspy tone to that of a high-pitched screech that is unrecognizable even to herself.[63]

Throughout my children's educational journey, they had to function in predominantly White spaces.[64] High school was a mixed bag. There were students of color, but for most of their higher track classes, they were some of the few minorities represented in those spaces. In high school, our youngest daughter was called the "N" word by a student in her physics class. Others referred to her as an "Oreo." This is a term used to identify minority students who seamlessly transition between both White and Black worlds.

In fact, because our daughter Miriam was a gifted student and talented athlete, she was considered safe to befriend. She was smart first, athletic second, and Black last. She recognized that as the reality of her daily existence.

Fortunately for her, she stumbled upon a group of young ladies who shared the same worldview as hers. They studied together and looked out for one another during difficult times. With these ladies, Miriam did not have to answer ignorant questions like "How are you getting to Ghana. Do you fly on

63. Harris, "Code-Switching," *Yes!*
64. Martin, "How to Thrive," Op-Med.

an airplane? Do all people in Ghana live in huts?" Some students thought that Africa is a country. These ladies were more informed about the rest of the world. They continue to stay in touch long after graduation from high school.

Life in college was, to say the least, a learning curve for the young Agamah ladies. Our daughters might be seated in a large room to study, but other majority students would peek in and refuse to enter the room because there were minority students present. During their freshman and sophomore years, they felt that they did not have the tools to address this issue. A six-week sojourn to Ghana in the summer of 2014 had a profound impact on the Agamah ladies' sense of purpose and self-understanding.

Once our daughters were in their junior and senior years of college, they felt empowered to do something about their situation. They got involved in leadership roles in predominantly minority organizations in their college. The Agamah ladies began to embrace their "otherness"[65] and created styles and fashion that reflected their African and Guyanese roots. In fact, they gathered a following of majority students who were willing and able to learn about their Black hair, Black hairstyles, and dress styles. They taught students how to dance and exposed them to other rich cultural diversity issues. They were influential in expanding the majority students' worldview.

I later learned about the term "empowered person of color," which describes a minority person who has an understanding of racism and its impact on them but chooses not to respond

65. John A. Powell and Stephen Menendian, "The Problem of Othering: Towards Inclusivity and Belonging," June 29, 2017, Othering and Belonging, http://www.otheringandbelonging.org/the-problem-of-othering/.

as a victim. Instead, the person rises above expectation and demands equal treatment.[66]

Miriam felt a clear sense of belonging when she joined the Office of Multicultural Development (OMD), an on-campus student organization for predominately international and minority students. All the minority people gravitated toward each other and found common ground upon which to stand. These students learned about each other's culture, food, and music. Miriam felt a connection and camaraderie like never before!

White spaces[67] trigger what is termed "impostor syndrome," a feeling of not belonging in an environment.[68] This feeling is felt by everyone, regardless of color or background. Our middle daughter, Aseye, experienced this throughout her time in graduate school. Moreover, minority students also have to contend with being "othered," which means a person becomes detached from the main body of a system.[69] This disconnect can negatively exacerbate and influence the quality of education that minorities receive.

Implicit bias is an attitude or stereotype that affects our understanding, actions, and decisions in an unconscious manner. Oftentimes, those in authority inadvertently contribute

66. "Key Terms ~ Race and Racism," https://www.vanderbilt.edu/oacs/wp-content/uploads/sites/140/Key-Terms-Racism.pdf.
67. Martin, "How to Thrive," Op-Med.
68. Kamal Sinclair, "Imposter Syndrome, Anyone? Oh, Everyone?" March, 31, 2015, Sundance, https://www.sundance.org/blogs/program-spotlight/imposture-syndrome-anyone-oh-everyone.
69. Powell and Menendian, "The Problem of Othering," Othering and Belonging.org.

to the inequalities in America's policies and practices toward minorities.

One sad example of this type of bias was explained to me by a minority medical resident, who said with tears in her eyes: "Although having grown up in predominately White spaces in school, my experience in medical school was difficult. I was one of the six Black students in a medical school of 600 students. Most of the time, the majority of the students would ignore us and would never have conversations with us. Making friends was very hard. I thought that maybe because my dad is a doctor and I'm from 'somewhere else' contributed to the alienation I felt. Most times, the majority students had practice sheets, they had information about exams and tests, yet we the Black students were left in the dark. I remember once confiding in someone in administration who noted that the reason myself and another Black student were unable to connect with the White students was because 'the two of you together was intimidating.'

"The experience almost broke me. And because of how hostile the environment was, it also created divisiveness amongst the Black students; we were pushed to the point of thinking we could not trust one another. I really felt alone."

Eli Goodman, in *The White Horse*, said, "The superficial fact that the melanocytes reside in the basal layer of the epidermis, yet, skin color has always been such an important determinant of our thoughts and actions. It even forms the basis of an anthropological theory, still advocated by some, that links race with brain size and intelligences. The advocates of this theory must assume that the myriad of genes involved in both intelligence and skin color are in close genetic linkage on one of our 46 chromosomes, an absurdity genetically, as well as ethically.

"Racism, however, is only one component of a pervasive refrain that has poisoned our minds through the ages. That refrain is our propensity to transform variations among ourselves, such as pigment, language, religion, and appearance, into the polluted veil of prejudice and hatred behind which we so often cower. It is true that differences among us give our lives and thoughts a welcome variety and interest. Surely, complete uniformity would be totally boring. We cannot, however, deny the fundamental truth that ultimately all members of our species are the same."[70]

In 1980, when Dr. Goodman wrote this article, he was on the staff of the Department of Internal Medicine at St. Mary Hospital in Philadelphia and was a clinical instructor in medicine at the Medical College of Pennsylvania. He was part of a team that harvested a deceased Black donor's skin in order to save the life of a White man. After four exhausting hours, their task was completed. He had overlooked the transformation that was occurring before him. The Black man was now White. And that's when it occurred to him that his burn patient, after his skin graft, was going to be 80 percent Black!

Color is indeed skin-deep. Because of society's labels, we often, do need to pick a side. The reality of our existence on earth is that all men and women are created in the image of God, our Creator, who has created humans in a rainbow of skin colors!

70. Eli Goodman, "An Illustrated Truth," in *The White Horse*, (New York: Morgan James Kids, 2016), 45–49.

Overall, unlike my young physician friend, I must submit that I am an empowered person of color since 90 percent of my encounters with people in White spaces have been the most rewarding and tremendously empowering experiences. Throughout my journey in America, communities of faith have been instrumental in saving me from drowning in the sea of poverty. I have been uplifted and encouraged by many during my wedding, then throughout my time as a student, and during my time in the workforce.

I have found that most people gravitate towards excellence. Those 10 percent who have wrongfully judged me by the color of my skin, I often pity. For they do not know who and whose I am.

True love in action seasoned with righteousness is the best combination. Every day, I encounter genuine people whose life purpose is to empower and enrich the lives of the poor in their local communities and abroad. Many of these beneficiaries of life-changing supplies, goods, and services would never meet or know of the countless hours these people in White spaces commit to saving unknown lives. They are the unsung heroes, the first responders of the globe, who sacrifice their retirement years to serve for a cause. They use their skills and talents to refurbish old sewing machines, make desks and chairs out of old pews, repair bicycles, and make uniforms and school bags for millions of children all over the world. Oh, how I wish I could name them here. But time and space will not allow me to do so.

One guy, Chuck, a retiree, captures it best. "I'm here to serve. Just tell me what you need me to do, I'll do it!"

Remember, 1 John 4:18 says, "There is no fear in love. Perfect love casts out fear. For fear has to do with punishment, and whoever fears is not made perfect in love."

* * *

We have come to know Man as he really is.
After all, man is that being who invented the gas
chambers of Auschwitz. However, he is also that being
who entered the gas chambers upright with the Lord's
Prayer or the Shema Yisrael on his lips.
—VIKTOR E. FRANKL:
MAN'S SEARCH FOR MEANING

Difficult Conversations

I had graduated from Bladen Hall Multilateral Secondary School the year before the Jonestown Massacre occurred. I was busy trying to figure out what my adult life would be like. While traveling on public transportation to Georgetown, I picked up a few murmurings from people around me.

"How come they allow so many people to come to our country and die?"

"What happen to them people, man, they drink poison Kool-Aid like da?"

When this tragedy occurred on November 18, 1978, most Guyanese people were not even aware of the existence of that many Americans in their country. In the 1970s, few Guyanese citizens had access to the television. We received information and news via radio and three or four major newspapers:

the government-run *Guyana Chronicle* and *The Gazette,* the privately run *Kaieteur News* or *Stabroek News,* and word of mouth. The news of the Jonestown assassination was plastered over the world.

The Peoples Temple and its leader, Jim Jones, a charismatic but paranoid man, led over 900 members of his "church" followers to commit suicide by drinking cyanide-laced Kool-Aid. How could that happen in my country, Guyana? This tragedy registered across the landscape quickly. The leader, Jim Jones, died from a gunshot.

My daughter Aseye was eight years old when I received a call from her school to come get her because she was ill. I was out shopping, so I made a beeline after checking out to pick her up from school. As we drove home, I heard news of the 9/11 attack on the twin towers in New York. Once we arrived home, I turned the television on and could not believe what I was seeing. We watched in awe as the series of 11 coordinated attacks by the terrorists caused 2,977 deaths and 25,000 injuries.

"What's happening, Mom? Where is that smoke coming from?" my daughter asked.

I recall looking in my daughter's questioning eyes as we wept together.

"Honey, I do not know why, but sometimes bad people do bad things to innocent people."

My little Aseye could not comprehend that people could fly airplanes into tall buildings. I wondered why this new "thing" was happening in America. This was surreal.

In 1978, when the Jonestown massacre occurred in Guyana, 918 Americans lost their lives. It could be argued that the Jonestown massacre was the second largest mass civilian deaths in this century.[71]

The question still remains, did the people of Jonestown take their own lives willingly or were they brutally murdered by insane persons? Perhaps the people of Jonestown could be classified as innocent or guilty of their own deaths. Most of the victims of the Jonestown tragedy were poor, disenfranchised minority Americans. Like me, they were looking for hope and purpose, a better life for them and their families. Jones, like the terrorist leaders, became a mastermind in control and therefore controlled the destiny of these nearly 1,000 souls.[72]

In fact, the people who died in the 9/11 attack went to work as usual. Some were mothers and fathers. They did not know that September 11, 2011, would be their last day on earth. Most of these victims were average, middle-class New York office workers. They could not conceive that such a thing could happen in one the most powerful and prosperous countries on the planet. Like most parents, I had no answers for the questions that swirled around the airwaves. Most of that time period, I kept the television off-limits to my children.

* * *

71. Michael Haag, "The Other 9/11," July 25, 2013, in "Alternative Considerations of Jonestown & Peoples Temple," sponsored by the Special Collections of Library and Information Access at San Diego State University, Jonestown.sdsu.edu, https://jonestown.sdsu.edu/?page_id=31986.
72. K. Harary, "The Truth about Jonestown," March 1, 1992, *Psychology Today*, https://www.psychologytoday.com/us/articles/199203/the-truth-about-jonestown.

You have the ability to choose which way you want to go. You have to believe great things are going to happen in your life. Do everything you can—prepare, pray, and achieve—to make it happen.

—Dr. Ben Carson

Catalyst for Caryl's Closet

Aseye is my second-born child. She said her first complete sentence at the tender age of 18 months. Her language acquisition was exceptional for her age. As she matured, she became the classic mediator between her siblings. She is the peacemaker in our family. Prone to be verbose, a discussion with her often had my head spinning.

"Mom, if you were given the opportunity to live without your arm or your leg, which would you choose?" she would query.

"Honey, I have to think about that."

"And how come we don't get to sleep over at our friends?" she would ask for the umpteenth time. Or "How come you don't let us call you, June?" and "How come we have to address adults by Mr. or Ms.?" Then that question would be followed by "Why are we the only ones in this subdivision and why didn't you all stay in Chicago?"

I would repeat the usual answers, but as the years went by, I knew I had to be less casual with my responses to her precocious ways.

The simple answers were that we are immigrants. We did not do sleepovers. The concept was alien to us. Why do our children need to sleep over when they have their own beds? We finally made a compromise and allowed our children's friends to sleep over at our place. Whenever my husband and I left town for a weekend away or to attend a conference, we allowed a select number of friends to host our children.

Over the years, I have regretted not being more amenable, considering her desires. It was not much later, Aseye became more reticent and did not engage in friendly banter with me, only with her sisters. She later confessed that she was looking for answers to her feelings of otherness. She could not understand why her mom was so different from her friends' moms. Being the only minority kid in her school, in church, and in most places, she often felt frustrated when she was among her peers. She wondered why her family was the only one of color in her subdivision. She felt lonely most of the time.

Then, one day, her life changed. *Essence* and *Ebony* magazines appeared in the mail. Her world suddenly expanded! Aseye was often the first to comb through the mail for these monthly subscriptions and headed upstairs to her room with them. She stayed up late at nights consuming the beauty and fashion of people who looked like her. This was transformational to her identity, self-expression, and sense of pride in her Blackness. "I would sneak out of bed," she'd say, "so that I did not wake my sisters, and I'd devour every page like it was candy!"

The first time she took a magazine to school and showed it to her classmates, they asked, "Why are all the people in that magazine Black? Where are the White people?" These images in the Black magazines reflected all kinds of beauty and broke down the hierarchies that she saw every day in her world. Her standard of beauty would forever be changed. Deep within her, she knew that she could dare be different! Aseye started designing her own style of clothing and experimented with her own unique fashion and wardrobe.

She described her dilemma and how she felt as she came of age in Springfield: "I loved to dress up but not like my contemporaries. I love music—all kinds of music—especially reggae, Bob Marley music, the blues, and calypso music. Actually, during my teen and early adult life, listening to music kept me alive. I often wondered, 'Why do my parents not listen to these cool rhythms?'"

I wonder why my mom never spoke about her Guyanese/ Caribbean soca vibes. I love this stuff! she mused. *I love dancing to all kinds of music. Why don't my parents dance? Every time I asked my mom about her past life, she changed the subject.*

Aseye continued her search for her own identity and meaning in life. She is, by nature, a curious individual. Her favorite pastime was to snoop around my closets, looking for interesting information. One summer, during her visit, she stumbled upon a scrapbook.

What? Is this my dad? How cool! My dad was so young, look at these funny comments!

She had found her dad's high school scrapbook. She was so excited. She could not wait for her dad and me to return home from out of town. She insisted that her dad explain every photo. She peppered him with questions about why he said that. And what did that comment mean?

Her dad smiled from ear to ear, then he said, "Aseye, life is too short. When I got to secondary school, I had to make a decision between being an average student or aim to be top of my class. I had to choose success. That's how I was able to make it this far."

Aseye spoke about finding her dad's scrapbook for months. She had discovered a piece of the puzzle to her existence. She had learned how to center the outside voices of her peers and landed on the reality that diversity was awesome! So, years later in her life, when she was looking for answers to her uniqueness, she stumbled on my photographs. She was determined to find out what her mom looked like as a baby and as a young girl.

Oh, look at these! Is this my mom? That's exactly the way I wanna look! Oh my! Oh my! That's why I'm the way I am!

Aseye had discovered "these treasures." She felt elated and empowered. She had asked the question in a number of ways: "Who is my mom?"

I had no knowledge of this seismic shift in her universe until my birthday that year. Aseye had worked meticulously for weeks to design a blog: Caryl's Closet: Ode to My Mother and Her Style in the 1980s.[73] This discovery fueled Aseye's thirst in search for building blocks to make a conscious commitment to fully own everything that made her who she was becoming. I was moved to tears as she showed me a display with commentary

It was author James Baldwin who said, "Children have never been very good at listening to their elders, but they have never failed to imitate them. They must. They have no other model."[74]

While in college in New Orleans, I had met James Baldwin at a discussion but had filed that information in the deep cre-

73. Agamah, *Aseye Says* (blog), "Ode to My Mother."
74. Jean-Phillipe, "Baldwin Quotes," *Oprah Magazine*.

vasses of my mind. Aseye found a large consignment of my
journals in my closet one evening during her search for relevance. In one journal entry, I had written about being in the
same room with James Baldwin and how I felt about meeting
him in person. I knew that Aseye loved reading. She loved using "big" words, listening to music, and writing in her journal
regularly. However, it never occurred to me to ask her who her
favorite authors were.

On the other hand, I had traveled extensively. I have lived in
many places and spaces and wrote excessively throughout my
journey. While growing up in Guyana, looking up words and
their meanings was my panacea for loneliness. I had created
my own dictionary of favorite words related to every subject I
took in high school. I loved to use unusual words in sentences
as I spoke to my best friend, Monty. He was responsible for
listening to each sentence and decoding the meaning of each
word. My compulsion to write about my experiences was evidenced by the stack of journals that Aseye had thrown across
my bed. I gazed at the distinctive cursive scrawls, the "ou" in
"colour" which gave evidence of my British-style education.

Who was this person? She obviously cared about politics,
societies and social norms, marriage, and family life. She had
argued for and against the effects of the use of inductive reasoning versus deductive reasoning. There were journals reserved for her spiritual journey. Then there were those that
focused on descriptions about places that she traveled to or
visited. Look! She had read most of E.B. White's and Norman
Mailer's work. She wrote commentaries on Tom Wolf and
Ellen Goldman essays. Yes! *She* was *me*! Why did I not major
in journalism at the University of New Orleans? That was the
proverbial question of the day.

"Mom, you need to be an author!" Aseye exclaimed.

For a greater portion of my life, I had immersed myself in learning about great writers and learning how to learn. However, it had never dawned on me that I could be considered an author by any stretch of my imagination! Was this disconnect due to my family values? I know that writing is an art. Some people would go as far as saying that writing is a science.

Personally, after the discovery of my journals by my daughter Aseye, I spent several days trying to decode my thoughts. My thoughts are many and jumbled. I have to force myself to think in a logical fashion. I have tried to brainstorm and extricate what information I had learned about writing from the greats like Joan Didion, Annie Dillard, E.B. White, James Baldwin, and others. I finally realized that a writer has to empty him/herself so that he or she could be a channel to bring forth important and meaningful stories. It sometimes takes a mind of steel and cups of tea (and/or coffee) to put his or her thoughts on paper.

And so it was, during the lonely hours of the 2020 pandemic, I had resurrected my thoughts, which had been laid to rest in my closet, and began to write my story, *Caryl's Closet!*

12.

Mission Dream

*Write the bad things that are done to you in
sand, but write the good things that happen
to you on a piece of marble.*
—ARABIC PROVERB

Edem told me before we got married that he would like to
use his gifts, talents, and medical skills to help the people in
Africa. He would like for us to plan toward developing some
kind of nonprofit ministry. Not only were we struggling finan-
cially, but now my husband was speaking about finding funds
to do something in Africa. My first response was "Why would
God take me out of poverty in Guyana, bring me to America,
and then take me back to Africa? Am I to be like Joseph in the
Bible?"

If you are familiar with the story of Joseph in Genesis 44,
you will remember, just like my forefathers in Guyana, Joseph
was sold into slavery by his brothers. In this story of God's
sovereignty, we are able to learn from Joseph how to trust God
through unbelievably difficult trials and temptations. Joseph
shared his dream with his brothers, about how he would one

day rule over them. They threw him into a pit and eventually sold him to some Egyptians. He ended up in an Egyptian prison. He was able to interpret Pharaoh's dream that there would be famine in the land. He became second-in-command to Pharaoh, and he stored up grain for such a time. Twenty years later, his brothers came to Egypt to buy grain. Joseph recognized them and decided to test them to see whether they had changed or were still dishonest people. Joseph deliberately hid the money they had paid in a silver cup in his youngest brother Benjamin's sack. After they left, he sent his men to bring them back in pretense that they had stolen the grain and did not pay for it. What followed next is a moving picture of God's heart of mercy and grace on Joseph's part. He forgave his brothers. He witnessed the transformation of Judah's heart as he tore his clothes and grieved the effect of returning to his father without Benjamin. They all dropped to their knees and repented of their sins then acknowledged their sins.

Similarly, we should all do the same. We are never alone, because it is God almighty who said He will never leave us nor forsake us.

I had to learn to trust and obey God as in Proverbs 3:5–6. "Trust in the Lord with all thine heart and lean not on your own understanding. In all thy ways acknowledge him and he will direct your path."

But what does trust mean? Does it mean that we should only trust God when we are in a bind? No, it means that we should commit our ways to the Lord as my forefathers trusted God and were rescued from slavery. My father trusted God when, at the age of 59, he left everything that he was familiar with to live in an environment where he had never experienced cold winter weather before, looking for better opportunities to care for his family. He had to learn new skills. He had to withstand discrimination, be disrespected, and shunned, all because of the color of his skin. My father had to endure the painful loss of his young wife, Walterine, at the age of 49, just two months after immigrating to the United States. He had no job or any form of medical insurance for her to continue to take her medicines after a major stroke in Guyana had disfigured her body. Two months after their arrival, due to lack of access to her medications, she suffered a massive heart attack and was buried in Slidell. With her premature death, all hopes of their American dreams together vanished!

My father had walked up and down the streets before and during Mardi Gras season, begging for a job. Any kind of work would do. He had bundled his narrow frame to protect it from the rigors of cold. It was his first experience of winter weather. He had felt the cold seep into his flesh from head to toe. That young fella who at the age of 14 years had strapped the old rag around his tiny waist. In Guyana, he had joined the older men, working toe to toe with them as they cut and hauled and punted sugar cane during harvest time. Then, much older in America, he was no match for this kind of cold. Someone had pulled him aside one day and schooled him in the art of layering, head covering and all. And as if looking well-dressed for the weather meant something, he had scored a part-time job, learning how to make paper mâché and then graduating to making Mardi Gras masks.

And before my parents, my Aunt Olga and her husband trusted God. They came to America in the early 1960s as missionaries. They came when a Black man and a Black woman could not sit at the front of the bus nor could they be served at a table in the restaurant.[75] But they came with a vision, and through God's mighty hand, they were able to accomplish many goals, including pastoring a Nazarene church successfully for over 15 years before retiring to spend their last days on earth in Slidell. They were able to bring all seven of their children to America, and today, those children and grandchildren have become prominent medical doctors, nurses, policemen, and productive citizens in this country. My Aunt Olga passed on her faith in the Lord to me and lead me to a saving knowledge of God when I arrived in the United States in 1983 under completely different circumstances. And with that, the torch of taking risks and trusting in God was passed on to yet another generation through me.

So was this God's perfect plan for me? Was this why He pursued me in my car on my way home from college on that winding lakefront road? I was beginning to get a clearer picture of what my purpose on earth was. I knew then that whoever said that "Success is never linear. A flat line means death. Life is full of peaks and summits; taking ups and flying downs; pleasure then pain; happiness and sadness; descents and ascents; going forward and then backwards" knew something about the vicissitudes of life on earth.

So once again, I decided to trust and obey the One who brought my husband and me together for a purpose. And so began our purpose together when Edem and I married in 1988. We led our first mission trip to Ghana in 1996, under the aus-

---

75. Sascha Cohen, "Why the Woolworth's Sit-In Worked," February 2, 2015, *Time*, history/#:~:text=1%2C%201960%2C%20when%20four%20 black,Supreme%20Court%20decision%20Brown%20vs.

pices of the International Health and Development Network (IHDN) and the blessing of our church, Hope Church.[76]

I fell in love with the people of Ghana. Their vibrant, joyful, engaging spirits reminded me of the people from my own village in Guyana.

Life back then was unbelievably rough. Imagine arriving in a poor village in the dead of night, after traveling for over 18 hours from America to Ghana. Our destination was to the village of Agbozume. A distance that should have taken three hours but took over four hours along a rugged, dusty, potholed roadway to get from Accra, the capital city of Ghana, to Agbozume, located in the Volta Region of Ghana.

The next few weeks in the village of Agbozume was life changing. Friends and family in the village came out to welcome our mission team with singing, drumming, and dancing. Every day we feasted on delicious Ghanaian cuisine, and as the evenings ensued, one by one, exhausted, we staggered to our guestrooms.

One morning, a "Durbar" was held in the center of the village. Local chiefs, queen mothers, important dignitaries, and community organizers celebrated the end of a year of good harvest and development in the village. There was no shortage of merrymaking, dancing, clowning around, and joy making late into the night.

The village of Agbozume, in 1996, had no doctors. There was only one midwife nurse and a number of witch doctors (or Juju men) and traditional healers. There were no telephones. Few homes had electricity, no running water in the

---

76. See International Health Development Network, http://www.ihdn.org/.

average villager's home. People filled potholes in the streets with garbage. It was a perfect textbook example for a budding public health student like me to learn on the job.

As a newly minted public health student, I took the opportunity to gather as much information about the health and socioeconomic status of the people of Agbozume and neighboring village of Klikor. This data was crucial to our nonprofit organization's efforts over the years. This baseline data provided a foundation to measure improvements in the health status of the people, the infrastructures, and the economic development in the community.

During the Durbar, someone said, "There is a doctor and his mission team visiting from America!" Those utterances were enough to change the entire atmosphere in the village. For the next four days, my husband, members of our mission team, and a handful of local villagers held clinic in a local village courthouse. We used bedsheets and cloth on the windows of the building to create privacy for patients. Our open suitcases were used as a pharmacy. Patients sat quietly under a mango tree on long wooden benches. For four days, we tended to patients to the best of our capabilities.

On the fourth evening, my husband became ill.

I was scared. He was the only doctor I knew, and he was sick! And to make matters worse, our three children ages five and under were with us. These little ones needed our care and attention. I had restless, intermittent sleep.

My husband and I knelt down to pray. We thanked God for seeing us throughout our experiment with mission work thus far and prayed for strength to continue the work. We were discouraged and reluctant to carry on. As we prayed, we sensed that God was not yet finished with us. During a period of quiet, I sensed the Lord's presence. *I love these people. You must love them more than things. I love people more than anything.* God had imprinted these things on my mind. It was just the beginning for us!

So this was another revelation of part of God's purpose and plan for bringing us together. The harvest was plentiful but the workers were few. We embraced the challenge that evening and never looked back.

Imagine traversing three continents (North America to Europe and Africa) annually for most of one's married life. During these 37 mission trips, with the help of US volunteers, we have trained, equipped, and encouraged hundreds of healthcare professionals, teachers, farmers, and construction workers in the Volta Region of Ghana. We are thankful for these volunteers who have accompanied us on these trips to and from Ghana over the past 25 years.

As a public health professional, one has to address the social determinants of health. Among these are, but not limited to, adequate housing, transportation, access to care (both physical and mental), and quality education, from kindergarten to college.

Meeting the needs of any community is nonstop. Support is needed to navigate the challenges. However, recruiting trusted people to work alongside us was difficult. Medical resources are few, hard to obtain, and expensive in rural Ghana.

A major part of our challenges over the years is that there was nothing for us to build on. In 2006, my husband and I made the sacrifice and purchased 23 acres of land in Weta, Ghana. We started construction of the International Health and Development Network (IHDN) Mission Hospital in Weta, Ghana, in 2006. We had to bring water and electricity from three miles away. We serve a catchment (outlying areas) of over 60,000 people. There was minimal support from the government of Ghana at that time. Efforts to raise support from the community was impossible. The average person in that community made less than $2 a day.

So where did the resources come from?

We had to take our lamentations to the God of the universe. We encouraged family and friends to support the work of IHDN. With support from family; friends; our church, Hope Church and others in Springfield; Laurel United Methodist Church; Moody Bible Church in Chicago; First Evangelical Lutheran Church in Decatur, Illinois; and many other partners, the IHDN Mission activities continue.

In 2012, I spearheaded the first Annual IHDN "Bringing the World Together" Fundraiser Banquet. Over the past nine years, with the help from our supporters, we raised over $640,000 in revenue to help fund the IHDN mission work in progress. This "Bringing the World Together" title was birthed from the variety of witnesses from many cultures brought together on our wedding day. Over the years, our annual fundraiser has become the talk of the town.

We live in the cornfields of White suburbia. This fundraiser features Ghanaian, African, Asian, European, and other cultures with the aim to once each year, showcase the world, its fashion, and vibrant colors. This fun and relaxing environment inspires people to give. We ought to remember that we Americans represent 75 percent of the world's richest people.

Many people came alongside us to support our fundraising efforts. It takes over 150 volunteers to host the annual banquet. I had to learn that in order to build a strong team of volunteers, I must see someone else's strength as a complement to my weaknesses and not as a threat to my position or authority. I learned to delegate tasks to these competent, talented, and capable volunteers. Over the years, my heart glows as I witness the growth and maturity of the young volunteers who started their life of service at the IHDN banquet. These people sacrifice time, talents, and their treasures to work for the betterment of people whom they may never see. Their efforts will not be in vain.

There is an Indian proverb that states "Where love reigns, the impossible may be attained." We also had to remain steadfast in the face of surmounting difficulties as we cared for others from a place of love. We began to witness the transformation of the villager's attitude as they recognized for themselves that they too can rise above their outward circumstances.

We kept hope alive through education and training and inspirational messages. For example, I have spent decades of my life imparting knowledge to teachers, students, community workers, and spiritual leaders. I have taught them how to overcome adversities and engage in community volunteer efforts, all while trusting in God. I often include in my messages the truth that we cannot control what happens to us in life, but we have control over how we will respond to our circumstances.

I often ended these training sessions with one of my favorite stories that best illustrates what life is about:

"Once upon a time, there were two male patients in a hospital room. Both men laid in their beds all day long. Every day, the gentleman closest to the window would describe to the other how beautiful each day was. He spoke about the different people, their families, the kind of clothes they wore, and the activities they were engaged in. He would report on the picturesque atmosphere down below and how he hoped and dreamed of getting out of bed one day to join them.

"The other man would look forward to hearing all of the wonderful stories and he too would dream of the time he would get better and experience some of the fun that awaited him outside.

"One bright sunny morning, the gentleman next to the window died. After his body was taken away, his friend requested that he be put in the bed next to the window. He settled in nicely and attempted to look outside, below his window. To his chagrin, all he saw was a tall black wall! He wept uncontrollably! He realized that his friend had a great imagination and wanted to cheer him up by describing beautiful scenes from his vivid imagination of what life could be."

I understood then that when we allow God to take residence in our imagination, we are engaging in providing hope for the people in our sphere of influence. We are His vessels. When we use our five senses to create beauty for others to enjoy, we are distilling parts of who God is. When we speak words of encouragement to others, we could literally change the trajectory of their lives.

The Ambulance Bid[77]

It was a bright, sunny Saturday in October 2014. My husband was on call that weekend. He called to ask me to do him a favor. He had forgotten that he was invited to the local Lincoln

77. Dean Olsen, "Used LLCC Ambulance to Help Patients in Ghana," December 29, 2014, *State Journal-Register,* https://www.sj-r.com/article/20141229/News/141229554.

Land Community College to attend a surplus property sale. He gave me instructions over the phone and told me to bid on an ambulance to be used in the IHDN Mission Hospital in Ghana.

"What! How do you do that?" I asked.

"I don't know, but we need an ambulance," he replied.

He told me to bid up to a certain price and then stop.

I arrived at the college grounds in Springfield. There were endless tools, equipment, office furniture, tractors, and trailers, you name it. People were following a gentleman from point to point, like the Pied Piper. So I registered for my bidding card and was given a number. I joined them in the bidding war. I loved listening to the cadence of the auctioneer's baritone voice. I enjoyed the rise and fall of his crescendo and the finality of his, "Sold!" I followed the pack until almost to the end of the sale, where the larger items were being sold. I casually walked over to where the ambulances were.

There was a young man sitting by one of the ambulances. I introduced myself.

"Hi, I'm June. Do you know much about this ambulance?"

"Yeah, this one's a Ford Cutaway Van. It has around 35,000 miles. The EMT students at Lincoln Land used this for years in their training. Still in good shape. What are you needing it for?"

"I'm looking for an ambulance to send to Ghana, West Africa," I replied. He moved closer to the ambulance, climbed onto it, opened it, and looked around.

"Yeah, apart from sitting here for a long time, it looks decent. Might need a new stretcher cover, but that's easy to come by."

I thanked him and moved on to look at other equipment for sale. Soon it was time to start bidding on "my ambulance." As soon as the bidding began, I felt my heart skip a beat. I was determined to win this! I waited until the third price, and I lifted my paddle. Someone else went higher. I waited out the next bid, then raised my paddle. I saw, out of the corner of my eyes, a tall gentleman raise his paddle and then slowly put his down again, not making a bid.

"Seventeen hundred dollars! Going, going . . . gone!" Through the flurry of everything, I heard the auctioneer's voice: "Sold!"

"June, you won the bid!"

I could not believe I had won!

I proceeded to join the long line to pay what was due for the purchase. The tall gentleman I was bidding against leaned over and whispered, "I heard you wanted to send the ambulance to Ghana. I wanted you to have it." He smiled broadly. And I returned his smile. It was a win, win situation. He handed me his card. "I buy lots of these items. If you need anything else to ship, contact me at this number."

That day, I learned a lesson about grace. That man represented what we all should strive to do. He did not know me. He just heard my story, and he was willing to extend a helping hand to a total stranger. He is now influencing the destiny of thousands of people, many of whom he may never meet.

With the help from the Midwest Mission Distribution Center, located in Chatham, Illinois, the vehicle was made roadworthy and shipped to Ghana.

The following summer, during one of our mission trips, we were standing outside our mission headquarters. I soon heard one of the sweetest virgin sounds in that part of the world. It was the high-pitched whirl of "my ambulance"! It had crossed seas, oceans, and borders. It was a welcoming sound.

Later that afternoon, our mission team gathered around the ambulance and gave thanks to the One who provides all good things! That ambulance joins a few others that are used for funeral purposes in the rural area in Volta, Ghana. However, the IHDN Mission Hospital has used that ambulance to save many lives already.

In October 2014, I was humbled to be recognized by the University of Illinois at Springfield as the winner of the Humanitarian Award for my work and contribution as an international healthcare advocate, organizer, and educator.[78] Then, in April 2015, my husband and I were awarded the *State Journal-Registrar* Finalist for the First Citizen and Legacy Award in Healthcare for our work in Ghana.[79]

Through the IHDN community outreach efforts, the Worgbato Elementary School and the surrounding neighborhoods have benefited from improved roads, drinking water, and reading materials to enhance learning. We are currently building a much-needed maternity and child delivery center in that village. This facility will benefit poor women who do not have quality prenatal and delivery services in that part of the community.

There is a Chinese proverb which says "It is better to light a candle than curse the darkness." Often, our destiny rests in

78. "Alumni Humanitarian Award," University of Illinois Springfield, https://www.uis.edu/advancement/alumni/awards/humanitarian/.
79. John Reynolds, "Julie Cellini Named *State Journal Register* First Citizen," State Journal-Register, https://www.sj-r.com/article/20151015/NEWS/151019686.

our own hands! We are the author of our own life story. When we act well, a shared joy is a double joy. And a shared sorrow is half a sorrow. We have no regrets about the sacrifice it takes to bring hope to others.

The author Edward Everett Hale said, "I am only one. I cannot do everything, but I can do something. And I would not let what I cannot do interfere with what I can do."[80] There is no other place in the world that I see this demonstrated year after year than whenever I go on mission trips to Ghana. Ghanaians use their bodies to carry and transport their precious wares, fruit, or whatever is needed to make a living. They walk for miles, often for hours, until the product is exchanged for the Ghanaian currency. They do not wait for someone to give them something. They are the hardest working people that I personally know.

The IHDN Mission Hospital Outpatient Hospital was opened in 2008. Then, in 2013, we constructed 100-bed inpatient hospital wards to accommodate increased patient needs. Over the years, the hospital outpatient department has seen over 30,000 patients annually. Every day, many deliveries of babies are taking place in the IHDN Mission Hospital. There is a vibrant community being built around the hospital.[81]

Today, after 25 years of prayer, planning, toil, and sweat, the Agbozume, Klikor, and Weta communities and surrounding areas in the Volta Region of Ghana have been transformed.

---

80. "Edward Everett Hale > Quotes," Goodreads, https://www.goodreads.com/author/quotes/8183.Edward_Everett_Hale.
81. Tara McClellan McAndrew, "Someone to Know: Dr. Edem Agamah Helps Improve Health Care Access in Ghana," *State Register-Journal*, https://www.sj-r.com/news/20180304/someone-to-know-dr-edem-agamah-helps-improve-health-care-access-in-ghana.

IHDN has truly played its part in making a difference in the destiny of thousands of people. Today, more people now have access to quality health care. With help from the Government of Ghana, most residents in the area now have access to running water and electricity.

My God Moments at Walmart

In October 2016, I had written this story in my journal:

I was in a hurry to rush in and out of Walmart off Veterans Highway when out of the corner of my eyes, I saw and heard the voice of a young Black man. He was sitting in a wheelchair. Next to him was a table with some books. I rarely look at people when I'm on a roll. I had checked off my to-do list and this was going to be my last stop before returning home for the day.

"Madam, can you help me, please?" came the voice clearly now. I stopped. Beckoning to a stock of books, he said, "This is my life story. I have sold many copies already."

He beamed. I could see the gold-plated teeth in the corner of his mouth. "Please buy one!" he pleaded.

I picked up one book, glossed through the title, and read the heading. "How much are you asking for your book?" I asked.

"Ten dollars, Ma'am!"

I gave him a ten-dollar bill from my wallet. Then he took the book, signed it, and returned it to me with a big smile.

"Here is my card. Please go online and make comments/feedback about my book."

And then, for the first time, I really paid attention to him. He seemed very sincere, and instead of sitting around, he wanted to share his story with the world. I was so touched that I asked him whether he would mind if I gave him a hug. His face lit up with another big smile as I reached over and gave him a hug.

But as soon as I crossed over the Walmart store entrance, the tears just gushed out of my eyes. These were blinding tears! The kind of tears that one might cry at one's daddy's or mama's funeral. The ugly type of tears. I was taken aback by the suddenness of the thing. I desperately tried to hide my tears as I fumbled through my purse for a tissue.

"What is this? Why am I embarrassing myself like this?" *I started praying to God for self-control.* "Please Lord, what is this about?"

Then it hit me like a blast of fresh air! I felt relief in my heart. I was too busy with my own life, and He wanted to show me that there are millions of young men out there that needed help, support, and affirmation from people like me, who have all my ducks in a row. God wanted me to feel for a change. He wanted me to look deeply and care.

I was not able to read the book until a week later. But I can tell you, I had never in my life read a more riveting, profanity-filled, and hard truth-telling of what millions of young people in the inner cities of America experience daily. A life of violence, drug abuse, betrayal, unrest, war amongst drug dealers and the police, and on and on. Most of what was written indicated that the goodwill efforts of the police to try to help some young men and women to stay in school, get out of violent situations, and stay out of prison was a daunting task. It is a vicious cycle! At some point I could not read this true story. I had to put it down. Yet I felt like I needed to continue reading.

For the first time in my life, I began to see and understand the insidiousness of that culture of crime and the horror of the cycle of poverty. His story spilled over to Springfield, which is considered a small, "safe" town. He explained that he grew up in Chicago. His home life was miserable. His mom kept being thrown in and out of prison and the authorities sent him and his siblings to school in Springfield to escape the gangs and culture of violence.

However, because the mold was already set, they could not stay out of trouble. They could not focus on their studies. They were sent from one high school to another but got caught up with chasing after girls, drugs, and guns. They reverted to the same lifestyle that they had experienced in Chicago. The young man ended up getting shot and thus having to be in a wheelchair for the rest of his life. He could never read a book from beginning to end until in his late 20s. The writer expressed great remorse over his actions, and he could not change his behavior until he gave his life to the Lord.

It was a very difficult book to read because of the profanity. For a country woman like me—a foreign-born, "educated" person of color—this experience was a stark reminder of how removed I am from the realities of the poor and suffering among us. I had to be reeducated, and the God of the universe saw that young man. He wanted me to see him also. For the rest of my life, I hope I will never look away when I see someone in need.

Thus, every time I sing the Matthew Ward song "The God Who Stays," I weep. I am reminded that the God who sees me, who runs in my direction when everyone walks away, is the real deal!

My second God moment at Walmart happened on December 1, 2016. I wrote about that in my journal as well:

Earlier in the day, I went to prayer group, but I left early before the session was over because I needed to pick up a few things from Walmart before going home to finish cooking dinner.

I finished shopping and stood in the checkout line. There were two people ahead of me. Another checkout lane opened up and the lady in front of me moved over to that line. I remained where I was, but I then became the second person in line. The lady before me had her supplies on the belt, so I placed a separator bar between hers and placed mine on the belt.

The lady completed her shopping and left. After checking my goods and supplies, the cashier said with a big smile on her face, "That lady before you said to give you this $50 to use toward your groceries/supplies today."

I was shocked. Then my shock turned to regret that I did not pay more attention to the woman who checked out before me. I looked around then, but she had already left the store. Here I was, not even deserving of such kindness. I did not need the money, but this complete stranger had offered to pay it forward. I needed to be able to thank her for her generosity.

She did not know me. It did not matter to her that I am a Black woman and she is White. She wanted to bless the next person after her. What an angelic act of kindness. I was filled with gratitude. I instinctively turned to the cashier.

"Ma'am . . . can I give you a hug?"

"Sure!" she said as she came around the checkout turnstile to receive her hug.

That day, I cried once more in Walmart as I gave her one of my biggest June hugs!

I left the store, convinced more than ever that that was a God moment. I had felt disappointed at first that I was the one in line to receive the $50 gift. But then I realized that I should be thankful and accept God's gifts that sometimes appear wrapped up in kind gestures by amazing people!

That experience left such an indelible mark on my life. I was doing the self-checkout at Sam's Club the other day. Out of the corner of my eyes, I sensed someone was looking at me. It was a lady and another elderly woman. I smiled. That was enough encouragement for her to cross the aisle and approach me.

"Where did you get your paper towels?" she asked. I could tell she was very disappointed.

"They are over in the far left corner of the store. You know, close to where the tire store entrance is," I said as I pointed in that direction.

"We looked over there, but there were none," she said.

I could sense her frustration and knew immediately what I needed to do.

"Here, you take mine!" I offered.

I could still remember the shock she felt, as evidenced by her facial expression.

"No, no problem, you need them more than I do."

She slowly and reluctantly crossed the aisle and I handed her the paper towels.

I do not know the details of the two women's story. Maybe they had looked many other places for paper towels before making the Sam's Club trip. What was clear was that they desperately needed those paper towels, and I needed to see their need and respond.

Culturally Confused?

Some people might say that I am culturally confused. I'm a product of all of Guyana, a country of six nations that has shaped me into who I have become. Honestly, I can identify with being "gray"—neither Black nor White. Because of the "gray" in me, I am unique. I can walk into a sea of White spaces and be comfortable. I can feel and identify with Indian, Chinese, Asian, European, and any other culture because I am a walking example of how these cultures can live together and coexist.

For the past 25 years of my life, my husband and I have trained and prepared mission volunteers, regardless of their ethnicity and talents, to serve in Ghana. We have never turned anyone away because of the pigment in their skin or their lack of gifts and talents. For we believe there is worth in every living, breathing person. We could learn from everyone, no matter their age or status in life. We have taken young children who have worked hard at whatever they were asked to do, without complaining, while some adults have complained unnecessarily about their environment.

I once listened to Pastor Ivan Myers teaching on "The Hidden Agenda Behind Racism." It was one of the best messages that I ever heard on this subject.[82] He read from Genesis 1:26: "Then God said, "Let us make mankind in our image, in our likeness, so that they may rule over the fish in the sea and the birds in the sky, over the livestock and all the wild animals, and over all the creatures that move along the ground."

His question is, "Did God create the human race or the human races?" He argues that "God created one human race." There is only one human race and the race was to reflect the image of God.[83]

---

82. Ivor Myers, "The Hidden Agenda Behind Racism," May 30, 2020, YouTube video, 1:15:25, https://www.youtube.com/watch?feature=youtu.be&v=zpEF8qa4pt4&app=desktop.

83. Myers, "Hidden Agenda," YouTube video.

What then contributes to the identity crisis in America society? It might be racial ignorance. You see, we do not take time to get to know each other. The only situation that I see this kind of comingling is on a sports team. Several of my friends told me that the most rewarding experiences that their children have had in college or high school were on the football or basketball team. It is the biggest equalizer when the students realize that their friends have the same passions and desires regardless of the color of their skin.

Moreover, when predominantly White cultures lack representation and exposure to other cultures, this results in ignorance of the beauty of otherness. The media and family traditions as well as the quality of education that American students consume on a daily basis contributes to the "us and them" mentality. The White cultural norms are often represented as the only right and best way to do life. These messages are projected in most arenas . . . whether it's the gold standard of what is beautiful in magazines or which ethnic group represents the greatest accomplishments in our society. How about the tossed salad mentality? The ingredients in a tossed salad are present in all of their individual flavors, but they are blended together to make this beautiful tapestry of vibrant colors and flavors in all of their glory.

I must submit that racial and or religious ignorance are learned behaviors and, therefore, can be unlearned with the acquisition of knowledge and truth. Often, one's ethnicity does not prevent one from receiving equality in educational or other opportunities to thrive in America. Some people may choose not to take advantage of opportunities given them because of ignorance or a lack of self-motivation. In that case, one reconciles one's cultural disconnect with what it takes to succeed in life anywhere.

In a recent conversation with my husband, he reminded me that God provided the air that we breathe to all mankind, whether we are rich or poor, Black or White. When we are in the same environment, we could never deny each other the use of that air. So why do we deny some the ability to have access to quality health care or food and water? For us, these issues of life have been the driving forces behind what we do as contributors to the welfare of the poor and the marginalized.

13.

The Reckoning: Childhood Memories

The truth is that all ethnicity reflects a unique aspect of God's image. No one tribe or group of people can adequately display the fullness of God. The truth is, it takes every tribe, tongue, and nation to reflect the image of God in His fullness.
—LATASHA MORRISON, *BE THE BRIDGE*

Easter in Friendship Village

My daughter Aseye called on the telephone to check in on us. She was away at college. We exchanged the usual pleasantries and shared information about how our week went.

She is our verbose daughter. She had to share line by line about her experience with her college professors. She spoke about the ones that made her feel comfortable in her skin and those she loved to avoid. She breezed on about her college life in exacting detail like a kindergartner after the first week of school. The sound of her voice was full of energy as words flowed like honey across a smooth surface.

Then she told us about her friend.

"Mom, Dad, I have this friend, she keeps telling me all about her travels to Guyana. Apparently, her parents take her there often and they have a fabulous time. I feel so silly, I told her my mom is from Guyana. Mom, do you think we could talk some more about Guyana when I come home for Easter?"

I told her, "Okay, have a safe trip home. See you soon!"

She hung up and I felt the tug of regret again. My husband commented, "We have been very busy over the years. She does not understand. We have so much responsibility on our heads! I wish they (our girls) would read more about these things . . . " His voice trailed off as he went back to reading his newspapers.

When the Agamah ladies came home for Easter break, I told them the following story:

"For the Christian, Easter is a time to commemorate the holy death and resurrection of Jesus Christ. Therefore, it is a time of celebration of Christ's amazing sacrifice for mankind, but for most Guyanese children, Easter was a time for flying kites.

"Good Friday marked the commencement of Easter. Most families attended church together and avoided eating meat. Only fish was part of the meal. It was considered a time of reflection; most people did not play loud music on their radios or cassette players. It was a calm, quiet holy day before the storm, when the celebrations began on Sunday. My mother, for example, made the slight adjustment and added extra sugar and raisins to the bread dough. Two pieces of dough formed a cross and a mixture of sugar and butter brushed lightly on top created hot cross buns.

"Every child dreamed of making his or her own kite 'from scratch' (or homemade). In those days, most people grew a Glama cherry tree in their back yard for such a time as Easter. Easter Saturday was devoted to kite making. Every family member would gather around the kitchen table. Our three brothers were masters at creating the kites. They were responsible for choosing the correct type of wood to make every piece of frame for our kites. They would ask permission of our dad to use his tiny tools to shave and painstakingly smoothen each piece of frame. We each chose what colors and type of kite paper we wanted; brown craft paper, opaque grease-proof paper, or the more expensive Barbados colored paper. We used the Glama Cherry glue-like substance or mixed flour and water to attach the paper to the frames.

"The frames and strings had to be placed just so. The nose of the kite was made from bamboo material so that it could bend into shape. Under the nose was the 'singer piece' (this was the white grease-proof paper which produced a singing sound as the kite rose in the air). The kite loops were essential parts of the kite. The mountain loop was the longest twines that connected from the upper right side and the upper left side and emerged to the center part of the kite. This allowed the kite room to be lifted by the wind. The much smaller loop, the pulling loop, attached from the ball of twine had to be placed in a certain way. This created more resistance on the face of the kite to the force of the wind and therefore gave you much more pull. And the length of the tail of the kite had to be perfect, for this determined whether your kite was 'top heavy' or flew smoothly through the air. This was no easy task. We stood, then sat, then jumped up and down with excitement as each phase of the construction progressed. This process sometimes took hours, and most times we went to bed late, dreaming of the sounds of kites flapping against the wind and waves lashing against the shore of the Atlantic Ocean.

"Easter Sunday was the time to wear your Sunday best to church. That was the time when women and young adults dusted off their hats and gloves to match their 'good' clothes. We children wore our Easter bonnets and laced gloves. Our mom would wash, comb, and braid our hair to perfection. Shoes were shined until they glittered in the sunlight. Families greeted each other and inquired about the children and grandchildren, and after church ended, people would linger, secretly admiring each other's outfits and giving open compliments to one another. Then people would remember the roast or chicken left in the oven and rush off to head back home for lunch.

"Easter time in Guyana was by far my second most favorite after Christmas. Our home, located about a one mile walk west of the Buxton-Friendship seashore, was a perfect location. By noon Easter Sunday, the main road in front of our home had transformed into this sea of colors, with the sounds of children giggling, laughing, and shouting words of admiration and commendation to each other as they held their treasured kites closely to their little, medium, or large frames. The adults carried ice chests and picnic baskets laden down with goodies, along with umbrellas for shade. This went on for hours, as it seemed at that time like the whole village had descended, headed toward the beach area of the Friendship Road seashore.

"There, on the shores of Friendship Village Seawall Beach, the greatest show began. As one neared the seafront, the sights of the array of colors arrested the mind like nothing else. The pulsating beat of the rhythmic steelpan music floating through the air did something to my little body and I started dancing to the beat of Reggae music or Calypso lyrics. Refreshment stalls, entertainment jungle jams for us kids, and the sounds of whistles and ringing from the ice-cream and popsicle sellers as they went by did not prevent us from reaching our favorite picnic spot. We laid our large blanket on the grass of the huge soccer playground, which was then transformed into a maddening crowd of kite flyers.

"Looking back on my childhood years of flying our kites, I do not remember any of our kites not 'taken to the sky.' That was testament to my gifted brothers who learned the art of construction from our father. Our brothers taught us how to fly our kites 'tall' to experience pleasure in creating something from scratch and enjoying the beauty of our creation as it soared higher and higher in the blue sky. They taught us how to recognize and avoid wicked kite flyers who deliberately put razor blades into their kite tails, so that on contact with other kites' tails, they cut them down.

"Throughout the afternoon, we dined on cheese straws, dahl pourie and chicken curry, chow mein, cook-up rice and channa, and drank mauby and pineapple drinks. When the sun went down, we lowered our kites, packed up our picnic baskets, rolled up our blanket, and headed home, knowing that the next day was Easter Monday!"

"Wow, Mom!" my girls exclaimed in unison.

Aseye stood up.

"You all remember when we were younger, Mr. David bought three kites from Sam's Club for us? We couldn't wait to fly our kites!" They all shook their heads in agreement.

Sarah lamented, "Yeah, we could not keep those babies in the air. Mr. David took us high on top of the Centennial Park hill. We tried returning the next day to fly our kites, but only Miriam's kite went up but came down with a 'thump'!"

"Hmm," I said, "I'm sorry . . . I recall how sad you all were. Those kites were poorly made. They were huge! Too top heavy. Nothing like the ones we made."

Christmas Time in My Village

It was Christmas 2017. My adult children—Sarah, Aseye, and Miriam—came home for Christmas break and, as usual, we gathered around the kitchen table to discuss plans for Christmas dinner.

My oldest daughter, Sarah, said, "Mom, what was Christmas dinner like in Guyana?"

I said, "Why do you ask? Well, it was lots of fun. Okay, let me tell you the story of Christmas when I was growing up. Maybe Christmas times have changed after all these years.

"Celebrating the birth of the baby Jesus and savior of all mankind tradition originated in Guyana when the Dutch first introduced Christmas in Guyana. Everyone celebrated Christmas, whether their religion was Hindu, Islam, Christianity, Buddhism, or otherwise. The entire country prepared months in advance. Christmas cards were sent out to family and friends a month before. Government workers, civil servants, police, and army men and women looked forward to receiving their Christmas bonuses and some form of salary increase. Guyanese traveled 'home for Christmas' no matter where they were, in country or overseas, because Christmas is a time for festivity and closeness of family.

"I have lived in a number of places in my lifetime but there is no Christmas like that of a Guyanese Christmas. I would submit that Christmas, the way I remembered it as a child, was the best time of the year. The atmosphere in Guyana would change like a soft blanket thrown over the whole country. People smiled more often and greeted each other with *'Season's Greetings!'* And parents seemed a bit gentler while reprimanding their children. Mothers and fathers reminded children to be good so that Santa Claus would bring them something good for Christmas.

"There is no Thanksgiving in Guyana to compete with Christmas season. So a month before December 25, every family gathered fruits and berries, ground them, and soaked them in Guyana Rum to make the Guyana Black Cake.[84] Christmas without black cake would be like having Thanksgiving without the turkey.

"People appeared happier and softer as they blasted 'Jingle bells, Jingle bells, Jingle all the way! Oh, what fun it is to ride in a one horse open sleigh . . .' from taxi cabs, on boom boxes, and from open windows. Steelpan bands and radio stations played Christmas tunes. Christmas carols were heard in every store and every public place, from banks to churches, far and near. Christmas lights glittered under the arches of doorways and streamed along decorated greenery up and down stairways. No matter your color, creed, or persuasion, Christmas functioned as the Balm of Gilead, and the entire country prepared for the greatest season of merriment!

---

84. Real Nice Guyana, "Guyanese Christmas Black Cake," December 3, 2017, YouTube video, 12:50, https://www.youtube.com/watch?v=5X3kKrdJBFU.

"As children in my family, we were responsible for helping our mother get the house in order before Christmas. We had to clean the floors, cupboards, and windows. The furniture was dusted and polished. Any torn furniture had to be reupholstered. The old curtains and blinds were replaced. My father would repair any loose boards, and all the wooden furniture had to be sanded and polished. My sister and I had to choose a new color to paint our bedroom walls. Our dad taught us how to hold the paint brush just so, to prevent making spills. My mom spent hours knitting and crocheting new chair backs and cushions. She would buy new tablecloths for the dinner table. We needed no other motivation to work hard other than the fact that 'Christmas is coming, so we have to be ready!'

"My father would choose one of the pigs to be slaughtered and prepared. My mom would salt the pork meat weeks before, and every day I had to carefully collect the chicken eggs because we needed eggs for baking pastries and cakes. Several of my 'chicken friends' would be sacrificed as well as ducks and meat bought from the butcher shop. All preparations had to be made and the home fully decorated by Christmas Eve. My sister and I would hang the new curtains and decorate the home with fairy (Christmas) lights. The black cake and sponge (white) cake had to be baked. The pastries (pine tarts, meat pies, buns, cassava pone,[85] salara, cheese rolls, pholourie, and roti) had to be baked and ready for the big day. The sound of Christmas carols could be heard all night and day, as each neighbor competed to outperform the other. There would

---

85. Real Nice Guyana, "Cassava Pone," YouTube video, April 1, 2018, 10:32, https://www.youtube.com/watch?v=2KHHCsbfJis.

be dancing and drumming in the streets, and the sounds of merriment could be heard far and near. No matter where our brothers were working in the country, they would be home for Christmas. Falling asleep on Christmas Eve was very difficult for my sister and me. We would finally fall asleep from sheer exhaustion.

"On Christmas morning, I would awake to the smell of Christmas as it punctuated my entire home. The familiar smell of pepperpot,[86] garlic, and roasted pork would fill my nose, and my tummy would grumble as I slipped out of bed. The scent of newly polished furniture, mingled with the smell of freshly baked breads, tarts, and other goodies, would greet me. Ginger beer, sorrel drinks, and pineapple drinks would be available to drink in abundance.

"We would gather as a family to give thanks to God for keeping us safe to enjoy another Christmas. My mother would serve breakfast. Breakfast consisted of pepperpot, eggs, salt fish, and homemade plait bread. We would drink strong chocolate milk tea and fresh herbal tea. In the background, we would listen to Christmas greetings on the radio coming from family members abroad who could not make it home for Christmas that year. I sometimes cried for the sad people who did not make it back home to enjoy Christmas in Guyana.

"The sounds of cap guns were heard everywhere—"

At this point in the story, my daughter Miriam interrupted, "Mom, what are cap guns?"

"A cap gun was the type of toy gun that gave off a light smoke when the trigger was pulled. Most boys wanted one for

---

86. "Pepperpot," African Bites, https://www.africanbites.com/pepperpot.

Christmas," I continued. "As for my sister and me, we would dream of having a doll that could walk and talk. We had to be content with a teacup set. We did not get a doll until we were much older.

"We were just happy to enjoy the sights and sounds of Christmas! There were masquerade dancers, men and boys who elevated themselves on stilts to perform amazing acrobatic dances. We threw coins for them to pick up and clapped when they succeeded. Members of the masquerade sang, 'Christmas comes once a year and everyman must have his share, poor Uncle Wiley in the jail drinking sour ginger beer!'

"Sometimes we attended church on Christmas Eve or early Christmas morning. The rest of the day was spent eating and drinking. My dad would take out his special whisky and Guyana Rum and friends and neighbors would pass by to say 'Merry Christmas!' and take a sip (drink). Then my mom would offer each visitor a slice of black cake and white cake. They would stay for a while and then move on to the next home.

"At last, the time for my favorite job had arrived. I loved that moment when my mom would call me to the kitchen: 'Caryl, come and share some of these cakes with the neighbors!' She had carefully wrapped parcels for every neighbor along our street: The Hope family, the Rutherford family, the Younge family, the McLennon family. . . .

"I took the woven basket and delivered the goodies with the biggest smile on my face until it was empty. Oh what joy, how I loved sharing with our neighbors! How I loved Christmas!"

Sarah said, "That's so beautiful, Mom! Why don't you ever make Guyanese food for Christmas? Let's do it!"

And so, for the first time in my grown children's lifetime, we had a merry Guyanese Christmas in our home in the corn-fields of Springfield!

Our Trip to New York (The "Big Apple")

New York is truly the city that never sleeps. It is the kind of city that I both love and then hate. It always takes me a while to adjust to the sights and sounds of the city. The constant movement and energy that pulsates there is almost jarring to my senses at first. Then within a few days, my senses catch up to things and I am okay.

I recall the first time I visited my sister Ingrid in Brooklyn. I was like a fish out of water. For the life of me, I could not keep up with the ebb and flow of how quickly one had to move. My sister took me shopping. The kind of shopping where we needed to catch the bus.

Before we were allowed on the bus, we needed tokens. Then we took the train, got off that train, then crossed over to the other side of the street and got on another train. These trains have numbers and letters. One has to stand on the correct side of the streets and avenues to make the right connections for the rest of the trip.

All five of my siblings reside in either Brooklyn, the Bronx, Queens, or Manhattan, all boroughs in New York. In August 2019, I took my middle daughter, Aseye, to Manhattan. My oldest daughter, Sarah, took a short break from medical school and joined us. We helped Aseye move into her apartment on the Columbia University campus.

During our visit, I took that opportunity to introduce my girls to members of my family. We spent one weekend at my Cousin Vashti's home. My children had met her during my dad's funeral in New York. Thus, our visit was to renew their acquaintance with their cousins.

During our time there, various members of my Guyanese relatives came by to visit. It was a convenient way to meet lots of people. We shared about "long time in Guyana," and my girls enjoyed listening to the cadence of the Guyanese accent. Several times during our stay, one of my cousins would speak to my girls in the Guyanese Creole language, but they did not know how to respond.

"Mom, how come you never speak to us like this? It's fun!" Another time it would be "Did your mom tell you all about your grandmother's cooking and baking?"

This kind of accusatory tone continued until I said, "Okay, I'm sorry, it's my fault. I have not done a good job in passing on the traditions of my Guyanese culture to the next generation!" I promised to do a better job from then on.

It was surreal to awake the next morning to the sound of our Cousin Errol, Cousin Vashti's husband, playing melodious piano music to "Clair de Lune" by Claude Debussy!

I walked into the kitchen. I was arrested by the sight and smell of my childhood experience of my late mother's cooking. I knew then that what I was experiencing was a gift to my children. So treasured. I was transfixed, transported back into my childhood moments of peace and comfort.

Cousin Vashti was preparing traditional Guyanese delicacies, made to perfection. I blinked back tears as I saw her season the rice for the black pudding as well as white pudding. Then she stuffed rice mixture into a casement to make it into a snakelike form. The smell of pepperpot (a traditional Guyanese stew) heating on the stove reminded me of Christmas morning when I was growing up. The soursop herbal tea boiling in the kettle did something to my insides. She was about to prepare a large bowl of souse (a condiment that is eaten with the black and white pudding). Vashti had already cut thinly sliced onions, cloves of garlic, celery, and other seasonings ready to be used in the Guyanese cook-up rice dish.

Looking at all these mouth-watering delicacies, I knew that Cousin Vashti had obviously started cooking early. The (beef and chicken) patties sat nestled artistically in a large plastic bowl. The sorrel drinks, ginger ale, and the maube drinks (flavored like root beer)[87] were already in their containers. And for a moment, I felt like I was back home in my mother's kitchen in Guyana, South America. But no, we were in Queens, New York!

This array of comfort foods displayed that day was part of the ties that bind the Guyanese diaspora living in the Big Apple. They came from Guyana, bringing with them their way of life and traditions. Unlike me, they had harnessed the best of their cultural heritage and packaged them to meet the growing demands of the younger generation. FOOD: It's the very essence of what makes a people of many nations one. The soul of the ingredients for their Guyanese traditional food could be found in the family stores, businesses, and restaurants in the Bronx, Brooklyn, and Queens. In every borough, there were open fresh vegetable and fruit stands, bakeries, and restaurants. There were signs, "Guyanese/West Indian," proudly displayed. These markets were some of the finest. There were definitely no food deserts in these communities.

---

87. A Google search for "Maube Drinks" generated more than 44,000 results.

I felt like people could afford fresh, healthy food any time of the day!

Of course, my daughters peppered me with questions. How did they get the ingredients to make all these goodies? Do they sell these in the regular shops or are there specialty markets for them? I attempted to answer. "There are a few of these traditional Guyanese food ingredients to be found in Springfield, where we live," I said. How did they get the tropical fruits in the United States? On and on they went.

In retrospect, I was very happy I had shared about Easter and Christmas with my daughters before our trip to New York. After a while, I just sat there and acquiesced to my cousins, giving them the honor of being the purveyors of wisdom to my daughters itching ears.

History Lessons on Guyana

In May 2018, our middle daughter, Aseye, completed her master's degree in English from the University of Illinois in Chicago. My family and I hardly had time to celebrate that night because the graduation ceremony ended late in the evening and most of the restaurants were full, thus we ended up getting carryout and heading back to our hotel rooms. Early the next morning, we caught a flight to Guyana.

Guyana is the only remaining English speaking country in the whole of South America.[88] Of the 13 countries in

---

88. "Guyana," Ge-It, https://www.everyculture.com/Ge-It/Guyana.html
https://www.google.com/search?q=Name+the+six+nations+living+in+-Guyana%2C+South+America&rlz=1C1SQJL_enUS810US810&o-q=Name+the+six+nations+living+in+Guyana%2C+South+America&aqs=-chrome..69i57.27903j0j7&sourceid=chrome&ie=UTF-8.

South America, there are nine countries that speak Spanish: Venezuela, Bolivia, Colombia, Chile, Argentina, Ecuador, Peru, Paraguay, and Uruguay. Brazil speaks Portuguese, Surinam speaks Dutch, and French Guiana speaks French.[89]

"What language are the people speaking, Mom?"

I explained, "Guyanese speak Creole, an English-based language spoken by the six nations brought together by the British colonists. These six nations currently living in Guyana are 'Guyanese,' formed by East Indian origin, 49 percent; African origin, 32 percent; Mixed, 12 percent; Amerindian, 6 percent; and White and Chinese, 1 percent."[90]

During our visit, my daughters and I were treated to a day trip to visit the Kaieteur Falls and the Kaieteur National Park.[91] We dined at the Banganara Island Restaurant and toured the evergreens with all their natural beauty. We spent several days sightseeing in Georgetown, the capital of Guyana. We visited the Stabroek Market, an outdoor marketplace. We passed by the iconic St. George's Cathedral, which boasts of being the oldest wooden structure that reaches a height of 43.5 meters. It is the seat of the Bishop of Guyana and was designed by Sir Arthur Bloomfield. It opened its doors on August 24, 1892.

We visited the Promenade Gardens located in Georgetown, south of Independence Park, the site of public execution of slaves who participated in the Demerara Rebellion of 1823. More than 10,000 slaves from the Demerara-Essequibo colony rebelled against poor treatment and a desire for freedom.

89. Ibid.
90. "Guyana," One World Nations Online, https://www.nationsonline.org/oneworld/guyana.htm.
91. A Bing search for "Kaieteur Falls Day Trip" generated 90,900,000 results.

Word had mistakenly spread to the slaves that Parliament had passed a law to free the slaves but that information had been withheld from the slaves. The rebellion lasted two days. A slave leader, Jack Gladstone at "Success" plantation, started the rebellion. His father, Quamina, and an English pastor, John Smith, were also implicated. Thus, the largest nonviolent rebellion was brutally crushed by the colonists under Governor John Murray. They killed an estimated 250 slaves.

After the insurrection was put down, the government sentenced another 45 men, and 27 were executed. The executed slaves' bodies were displayed in public for months afterwards as a deterrent to others. Jack was deported to St. Louis after the rebellion, following a clemency plea by John Gladstone, the owner of "Success" plantation. John Smith, who had been court-martialed, was awaiting news of his appeal against a death sentence; he died a martyr for the abolitionist cause. News of Smith's death spread to Britain, and this strengthened the abolitionist movement in Britain. After Guyana's independence from Britain in 1966, Quamina was declared a national hero for starting the rebellion. A number of streets and monuments in Georgetown have been named after this brave hero.[92]

Life in Friendship-Buxton Now

We observed what the modern-day life of Buxtonians was like. Modern-day life and the rich traditions in the village still go on. People are still very friendly and engaging. Men and women continue to work hard to make ends meet, no matter

---

92. "Demerara Rebellion of 1823," Wikipedia, https://en.wikipedia.org/wiki/Demerara_rebellion_of_1823.

what. They are still outgoing people. Life is calm. There is a tranquil gentleness in the village life.

People greeted us as we walked through the village. "Caryl! Is that you? Man, you're all grown up!"

"I remember when you were in my class. Where are you in the States?"

I would often reply, "I'm around the Chicago area." No use saying, "Springfield, Illinois." No one knows where that is, but everyone knows Chicago and New York.

The thing about my village is that it's real community. When I came to the United States, churches always talked about *building* community. In Guyana, *community* is the fabric of all they do. People from the village look you in the eye. They greet you warmly.

The thing about it is, you don't have to physically be there all the time. When you return to visit, you pick up where you left off . . . as if you were never gone. After a few days, your speech turns into the singsong patter of the "Guyanese twang." You laugh a bit more easily as friends greet you, "This time na like lang time." Meaning things have changed for the better. We do things differently from the way we did long ago.

But do we *really*?

When I was growing up, everyone knew about everyone's business. When someone was leaving to go abroad to further their education or to start a new life, we would all dress in our fine dresses and suits and go the airport to see them off. We would make the trip into a family excursion. Long after our family member or friend boarded the aircraft, we would all wave goodbye and shoot kisses in their direction. Then, with a sense of relief, we would head back home to our daily humdrum life in the village.

You greeted people by asking how the family and children were doing. No one ever said, "I will be praying for you." You knew that they genuinely cared for you and every member of your family's success. When a villager succeeded in his or her exams, it was everyone's victory. We cheered for the whole family. If a boy or girl behaved "badly," mothers engaged elders in the village to "speak" to them. That might mean a "talking to" or a spanking as a form of counseling. We knew when someone had a baby and who got married. People did not need an invitation to "pass by" to see the baby.

When someone died, the death announcement was heard on the radio. No invitation was necessary. People would come by and sit with the family. As new visitors arrived, the previous visitors would leave, and like musical chairs, family and friends would revolve in and out sharing their care and compassion until late into the night . . . often into the next day.

When my father died in the United States of America, we flew his remains to Guyana. Even though my father had spent many years abroad, on the day of his funeral it seemed like the whole village showed up.

Most Guyanese love to cook. They are generous with sharing food and meals. Visitors will bring fresh fruits and herbs from their yards. They shared time and themselves with you. They reminded you not to forget where you came from. It is implicit. No matter where you roam, you must always remain a Buxtonian.

If I were to take you to Guyana today, you would feel safe. We could walk down the Buxton-Friendship street for miles, then stop by the coconut seller's stall and drink a freshwater coconut to quench our thirst. We could walk in the dark, flashlight in hand, holding hands for support, and not fear being attacked by anyone. In America, I learned quickly that one cannot let one's children out of sight. When I was a child, I could play outside until dark and not be afraid, that is, until someone snuck up from behind and scared you!

When we arrived at a friend's house, knowing there was a dog in the home, we announced our presence from afar. "Upstairs, is Carl home?" Often the residents would hear the dog bark and look out the window to see who was there. Then, once you were invited in, you would remove your shoes and leave them at the entrance of the door.

That custom has practical roots. Because most people walked to their destination, their feet got dirty. Families mop their floors every morning. So taking one's shoes off is a sign of respect.

During our family's visit to Guyana in 2018, most people from the village of Buxton-Friendship were employed in Georgetown by the government of Guyana. They were employed in the fields of education, healthcare, public service, and law enforcement. Several people were self-employed as independent building contractors, electricians, in furniture manufacturing, and trade services. Others provided car and bus transport services, food vending, beauty, and hairdressing services. There were a number of enterprises, such as farming and livestock and fishing. Vegetables and fruits abounded. People ran bars and small cafes. The largest bakery shop in the community is located in Buxton and has several branches in Guyana. Benjamin's Homemade Bakery was thriving. There were pawnbrokers and jewelry shops and clothing and hardware stores. There were many locally owned businesses.

All public main roads and small streets were paved and lighted. However, some of the trenches were overgrown with weeds except for the Company Canal (the body of water that runs east to west throughout the village). It was dug in 1886 to provide irrigation and drainage for the farmlands. It was clear of weeds and well-maintained. This canal separates Buxton and Friendship. Some village youths were frolicking as they ran around and pushed each other into the pale gray-ish-brown body of water.

The community still has a government-run post office. Much work needs to be done on that eighteenth century-style structure. There was a privately run wholesale beverage distributing business, a gas station, and several other privately run shops and stores.

Buxton Health Center is a primary health care facility that provided emergency medical and dental care. It was staffed by a physician, pharmacist, nurses, assistants, and other support staff. However, the need for maintenance and upkeep on the building was still the main challenge for the village people. The top portion of the building was in need of repair. Most of the roads and walkways were paved, so riding a bicycle was easy. Several bicycle repair shops were plying their business.

Young men and women were encouraged to get involved in community development and sports activities such as cricket, soccer, football, track and field, circle tennis, cycling, volleyball, and basketball. There was a Soccer Club. Young men were also engaged in the local Cricket Club that promoted and organized events. Most of these gatherings were held in the Village Tipperary Hall. My husband and I witnessed the reorganization of the Buxton-Friendship Village Steel Band by a retired gentleman, who is a community organizer. He was resurrecting this traditional music art form to pass on to the next generation. Today, this vibrant steel band has won various awards in the county and elsewhere.

The church continued to be a major part of the fabric of the Buxton-Friendship Village life. The historic St. Augustine Anglican Church was my mother's church. It still stands in its pink-with-white-trim glory, a picturesque sight against the backdrop of a tall green grassy marsh. When I saw it, I was in awe because of its quaintness and beauty. This church was established in 1855 and opened its doors for worship on Sunday, August 1, 1856. The Buxton burial grounds next to it were well-kept and manicured.

While we were visiting, my husband and I attended the Friendship Methodist Church. This was my father's church. We observed that most of the congregation were young people, but I did recognize some elderly people from my past years of attendance. My sister Ingrid and I went to church and Sunday school there every week and went to confirmation classes there for six weeks. Very little had changed over the years. I recall, as an adult, I returned to attend a funeral there. It was very hot and crowded. I felt faint and almost passed out. But I didn't.

Although Buxton has shed much of its eighteenth- and nineteenth-century architectural features, there are some impressive homes, shopping areas, and vibrant business popping up around the community. Most homes built in the early 1960s sagged under the weight of aged Greenheart wooden posts. The rusted brown aluminum sheets on rooftops contrasted against white wooden structures and revealed the time of construction of those homes. Some homes were built with shingles once white, now rusted dark brown or cream, and their wooden steps creaked under one's weight. Some still held wooden jalousie windows, broken in several places but held together with pieces of wood. But right next to those homes, we saw larger modern, colorful concrete structures. The bright pink, yellow, green, white, and cream two-storied structures stood out like monuments to a testament to modernity. These homes were fortified by tall concrete fences that were interwoven with barbed wire on top to prevent the unwanted entrance of a burglar. The famous Tipperary Hall of Buxton, a meeting place for village social activities, dances, and celebrations, was newly renovated and still an important hallmark of Buxton pride.

I was disappointed when I saw the once magnificent Buxton High School building had aged. Its once stately posture was beginning to sag under the weight of old age. The once lily-white paint was then turning gray. The windows were broken in places. The blue sign, "Buxton High School Library," is still affixed in front of the now worn second floor of the building. I felt like weeping. That space once held a special place in my heart, the library. Should that building disappear like so many others, I would be heartbroken!

However, there were signs of community engagement in the restoration of the Buxton-Friendship legacy. In 2018, the Buxton-Friendship Restoration Committee was formed in New York. Its main goal is to encourage citizens of Buxton who reside in the diaspora to give back to the village by volunteering, donating, and sharing their gifts and talents with the locals. The diaspora are groups of families who originated from Guyana and now reside overseas. They live in North America, Canada, England, and West Indies, etc. This Buxton-Friendship Heritage Group keeps us updated about events and features scholastic accomplishments by Buxtonians in-country and abroad.

Each year, they host the Emancipation Commemoration with weekly activities that serve to engage the community in participation in church services and senior citizen's parties. During these events, the oldest persons alive in the village are recognized and celebrated by everyone. This celebration includes arts and craft shows, fashion shows, and cultural shows that showcase the traditional dress and stories that are passed down from generation to generation. Steelpan music and dancing are staples at this annual event. Lectures given about the history of Buxton share the struggles that our ancestors went through and the challenges our youths face today. Cultural camps for the youth and excursions (picnics and trips by buses and cars to historical museums in Georgetown and other historical villages) are offered.[93] The goal is to share and keep the village traditions alive and pass these on to the next generation.

Recently, in 2018, the Buxton-Friendship Museum was established in Buxton. This is a nonprofit organization that seeks to collect, house, and display historical artifacts and information on the history of the Buxton-Friendship Village. On August 1, 2020, Guyana celebrated its 182nd Emancipation Day, commemorating the day slavery was officially abolished in Guyana.

---

93. Victoria Uwumarogie, "What's Going on, Chap," January 8, 2015, Madamenoire, https://madamenoire.com/501475/wah-goin-chap-9-celebrities-probably-didnt-realize-guyanese/2/.

It Takes a Village

There are a lot of things I do not understand about life. Things like why one person dies young and the other lives to old age. I don't know why people do harmful things to innocent people. But I know there is a God who sees me and knows me.

There are a number of lessons I learned along the way as I journeyed through life from Guyana to Barbados to the United States and the country of Ghana. I have experienced grief, loneliness, rejection, and discrimination. Yet I was filled with determination. I heard the voice of God clearly and experienced God's abiding love. I have learned the importance of daring to be the outlier (moving in predominantly culturally different spaces,[94] unlike the ones in which I grew up), in order to be in God's perfect will. There is no license for expressing kindness, love, and compassion toward others. My spirit has been lifted up by gracious unsung heroes throughout my sojourn.

I have lived in Springfield, Illinois, the longest. Living in Springfield for over 25 years has taught me that people generally want and admire excellence and good deeds.

I remember shortly after we moved to Springfield from Chicago, I went shopping at one of the local grocery stores. I did my shopping and headed home.

My home phone rang and I picked it up.

"Is this June Agamah?"

"Yes, this is she."

---

94. "Sociology," Yale, https://sociology.yale.edu/sites/default/files/pages_from_sre-11_rev5_printer_files.pdf.

"Ma'am, someone found your purse in the shopping cart and brought it to our customer service department."

I could not believe things like that happened anywhere!

"Wow, thanks! I'll be right there to pick it up."

Over the years, our children were involved in a number of sports and academic pursuits. Their photographs would often appear in the local *State Journal-Registrar* newspaper. I cannot tell you the number of kind, caring people who took the time to cut those clippings out and mail them to us. Our children would often receive encouraging notes from the congressmen, and some of my husband's patients would remember our children and their accomplishments long after they had grown up and left Springfield. It did not matter that our children were often the only minority students on the pages of the newspaper. Being the only one on the page or in the room means they are overcomers. People genuinely rooted for them.

Years ago, when my husband shared his desire to do mission work, our senior pastor at Hope Church recommended the right people that were knowledgeable about setting up a nonprofit organization. People in the Springfield community have rallied around our family and have volunteered and supported the work of IHDN over these past two decades.

As I read Roy T. Bennett's *The Light in the Heart*, I agree with his words: "Always remember people who have helped you along the way, and don't forget to lift someone up."[95]

---

95. "Roy T. Bennett Quotes," Quote Catalog, https://quotecatalog.com/communicator/roy-t-bennett.

Love Is the Game Changer

Another lesson I have learned is that love is a game changer. I have traveled extensively. I have been to many events, familiar and unfamiliar, welcomed and unwelcomed. Whenever I walk into a room full of people, when I start giving instead of waiting to receive, I always get back. Whether it is a warm smile, a sincere "Hello, there," or a warm embrace or hug, it's amazing what happens in the room. With every action, there is an equal response to what you put out. I choose to put out love. Love has never failed me. It is the most powerful force on earth. Love can scale walls, climb mountains, and walk through valleys. Let your love shine so that others could give glory to the God who placed you on this earth to be a difference maker.

People are the same everywhere. We all need love. When we are patient with others, we are able to see beyond their faults. When we are kind, we disarm those who are not. When we express genuine humility, people recognize that and are willing to share their darkest secrets with you. And when we give God the glory He deserves, we are living out the faith we have been given.

I realized that for me to understand who I am and how I got to here, it's clear that I needed to understand my history. And that history must include the contributions of my African ancestors and their descendants to my story. Not that this has to be a separate story, but it is about demonstrating that the African story has been intertwined with the European's and all the other nations around the world. It is a story well worth telling. This is the story about how *Caryl's Closet* came about!

And finally, can you just imagine with me for a moment? You and your children and grandchildren along with me and my children: We are in a gathering representing a multitude of all nations. We join our hearts together to share the rich stories of our journeys.

What a joyous celebration!

4. Which themes seems more prominent when you consider ways to form relationships and interact with others?

5. In Philippians 1:12-15, Paul is in prison but he rejoices. List people you know who have endured hardship yet they seem full of joy.

6. What events or situations in your life has been the hardest to share with your loved ones? Are you encouraged to share these experiences now?

14.

Extras

I've got a general callout with the Caribbean world in which I'm interested in helping in any way to get their well-written good stories out to the rest of the world. I am really interested in helping those stories get to a completion and public viewing.
—C.C.H. POUNDER

When we have culture gaps, sometimes it is best to give you, the reader, the background needed to prevent you from feeling lost. Below is just some information to help you as you travel alongside me in this journey.

My first name is June and my middle name is Caryl (Kahril). Most of my life in Guyana, up until I came to the United States, I was known as Caryl.

I use the term "Buxtonian." This is the title for all people born of ancestors from Buxton-Friendship Village, where I was born.

British Guiana became Guyana in 1966 after Guyana gained independence from Britain.

All people born in Guyana in 1966 and onward are referred to as "Guyanese." As of 2011, there are 208,899 Guyanese born immigrants currently living in America. A majority of them reside in New York City.[96]

Famous people, like actor Derek Luke, were raised by Guyanese parents in New York.[97] The famous Carol Christine Hilario Pounder is also a Guyanese-American actress who appeared in the role of Dr. Angela Hicks. She was born on a plantation in Georgetown, Guyana.[98]

Guyanese people represent six nations brought together for one purpose; to make money for the colonial masters. Amerindians, Africans, Indians, Europeans, Chinese, and Portuguese are the major ethnic groups.

The names of the foods, vegetables, and places were derived from the different people groups and countries that occupied Guyana and the plantations in the country. Most of the fruits and vegetables are tropical in nature and would be named differently in other Caribbean countries. For example, the Guyanese national dish is "pepperpot." This dish was introduced by the indigenous people group Arawak, Carib, and Warrau. The "metemgee" seems to have its origin from Africa. The "Guyana Black Cake" has its origin from the British plum pudding with the addition of Guyana Rum and molasses.

---

96. "Guyanese Americans," Wikipedia, https://en.wikipedia.org/wiki/Guyanese_Americans.

97. A Google search for "Derek Luke Raised by Guyanese Parents" generated 765,000 results.

98. Guyanese Girl, "She Rocks: Meet Carol Christine Hilaria Pounder (CCH Pounder), Film & Television Actress," October 4, 2012, Guyanese Girls Rock, https://guyanesegirlsrock.com/carol-christine-hilaria-pounder-actress/.

"Stabroek Market," and "Essequibo" were named by the Dutch. "Georgetown," the capital of Guyana was named so by the British colonists. The French also named forts, like "Fort Nassau," and so on.

"The Jonestown Massacre" occurred in Guyana in 1978. I was 18 years old and coming of age then. This incident put the country of Guyana on the map for the first time.

I use quotes in my memoir because they represent some of what I have experienced over the years of my maturation.

I use references to enable my readers to get access to any unfamiliar places, stories, and video recipes for some of my favorite foods.

The "Black Table" is the table in most predominantly White American schools where minorities sit to become insiders.

"Code-switching" is a term used to describe how minorities try to fit into the corporate world. It is how they survive in these environments.

Some other terms of note include:

"White Spaces": Blacks perceive settings and neighborhoods where schools, restaurants, workplaces, and other spaces are off-limits to people of color.

"Black Spaces": White people typically avoid Black spaces, but Black people are often required to navigate White spaces as a condition of their existence.

"Outlier": This is a non-White individual who moves in predominantly White spaces.

"Othered": The view or treatment of a person or group of people as intrinsically different from and alien to oneself.

"Token": Individuals are deemed tokens when they enter a job environment in which their social category (sex, age, etc.) historically has not been.

"Implicit biases": Implicit biases—attitudes or stereotypes that affect our understanding, actions, and decisions in an unconscious manner—often influence and create inequalities in our programs, policies and practices.[99]

"Societal biases" or "Social biases": Also known as attributional error, social or societal bias occurs when we unwittingly or deliberately give preference to (or alternatively, to look negatively upon).

"Cultural biases": These can be described as discriminative. There is a lack of group integration of social values, beliefs, and rules of conduct.

---

99. Kirwan Institute, The Ohio State University, "Understanding Implicit Bias," Kirwan Institute, http://kirwaninstitute.osu.edu/research/understanding-implicit-bias/.

Acknowledgments

Caryl's Closet has been a journey of faith and love and will propel me to greater heights of understanding of who I am. Writing this memoir has already done so much for me, because it has brought me back and center to my rich African and Guyanese roots.

This book-writing journey has been bathed in prayers. I must confess that the process has been a life-changing experience for me. I felt buoyed by everyone's prayer that this work will be written from my heart to yours, my readers. Thus, please accept my sincere gratitude to all those who have been a part of this journey with me.

To my family: Thank you for your enduring support in allowing me to share parts of our family life with the world. Although so much of what we have done as a family is well known in our local community, this has been a stretch. Aseye, thank you for persistently asking the hard questions and being patient with me. Thank you for encouraging me to write. Your inspiration will always be the best validation that I received from anyone in a long time. I was honestly not aware that my life had much significance until you pointed me in the right direction.

As members of my family, you have always been busy with school and work, but you have taken time and effort to encourage me during this season. Sarah, Aseye, and Miriam, thank you for listening to me read parts of my story to you and helping me edit my thoughts when necessary. My hope and prayer is that this book will bring us closer together and ignite healing and understanding of who you are, where you came from, and where you are heading.

To my brothers and sisters: Ours is a story that needed to be told. Our parents were examples of results of what hard work and discipline can accomplish in life. Ingrid, thank you for being my big sister and memory bank. You made difficult times, laughable ones. You and I were a team that made sacrifices for one another as young children. When times were rough, we paved a way to make life bearable for each other. My brothers, thank you all for being our cheerleaders and defenders when we needed you most during our younger years. Thank you, Nola and Ingrid, for your listening ears to my early writings and remembering with me the details of our childhood journey together in Guyana. I hope you all know that without you, I could not have a story. And thank you all for allowing me to share a part of your lives with others.

To my relatives: To all my cousins, the Guyanese-Americans who first knew me as Caryl (Kah-ril). Thank you for being a central part of my journey. When I had nowhere to go in New Orleans, you housed and fed me. As Desmond Tutu said, "My humanity is bound up in yours, for we can only be human together."[100]

---

100. Irwin Kula, "10 Pieces of Wisdom from Desmond Tutu on His Birthday," October 7, 2013, The Wisdom Daily, http://thewisdomdaily. com/?s=10+Pieces+of+Wisdom.

Michael and Towanda Schultz, Jr., thank you for keeping our family connected via Zoom. Thanks to Dr. Gaa Dawn Schultz; Sonja McGowan; Cousin Eunice Schultz; Esther Schultz Connor, author of *The Mighty Seed*; Dr. Grace Schultz; Viola Facey-Schultz; Michael Schultz; Joyce Schultz; Clifton and Mariana Schultz; Wayne Conner; Mark Schultz; Michelle-Ann Gibbs; Sharon Gibbs-St. Stanislaus; and Cousin Christina Thomas-Gibbs. And to all the others that are not mentioned here, know you have been instrumental in believing in me.

To those of you in the New York area, thank you for helping me to remember where I came from. Thank you, Cousin Errol and Vashti Cockfield. You have been mentors for my sister Ingrid and me since our teenage years. Errol and Vashtie, you have demonstrated how a married couple should love and support each other. You have been the glue to hold the Guyanese diaspora in New York intact over the years.

To Kenrick and Diane Chance: You always show up, ready to serve and make things happen. Thanks to Errol Jr, and Ziedah Cockfield for making us feel at home away from home. My daughters have found in all of you the foundation that they so yearned to experience: the Guyanese culture that is still intact in the Big Apple.

To all my relatives in Springfield: Ms. Hilda Elie Ahiable, Eyram Tettevi, Joy Tettevi, Emma and Clemence, and Makafui Ahiable and family. Life in Springfield would not be the same without your support.

To my friends: A great thank you to my dear friend and honoree editor-in-chief, Dianne Poe Pickett. You were the first to be brave enough to believe that I could do this. Without your dogged persuasive and quiet persistent promptings, I could not have accomplished so much in a short time. Thank you for the countless hours of FaceTime and Zoom calls, prayers, and sisterhood. Your ability to pull out more of what I wanted to communicate, along with your piercing follow-up questions, is remarkable. Your insight into human psychological makeup has allowed me to flesh out my thoughts more clearly.

Dianne, I so appreciate you introducing me to your wonderful literary-minded friends. They listened to my stories and made suggestions about fine-tuning things. You introduced me to your wonderful friend, Joni Sullivan Baker, managing director of Buoyancy Public Relations, who in turn connected me to my wonderful publishing team with Carpenter's Son Publishing and Clovercroft Publishing. Thanks, Jim Pickett, for putting up with me and making light of every phase of the journey. Jim, you are one of the most fun-loving persons that I know. Thanks for your prayer support. And Jim, thank you for always making what could have been a burdensome effort, fun.

Thanks to Claudia Kirby, my neighbor and cheerleader. Those scheduled, middle-of-the-day, sitting on the couch, tea-time readings were the best! I enjoyed reading my work to you watching your face light up as you related to aspects of my story. For all of you who came by to lunch and endured my reading to you: Amy Gelber; Sharon Johnson; Kim Dunnington; Ryan Williams; Liz Eilers Bron; Polly Danforth; Angela Severado; Dr. Nicole Abbot; Dr. Nana Cudjoe; Dr. Oritsegbubemi Adekola; Dr. Jennifer Addo, blogger; Lin Vautrain; Dr. Saira Silas and family; and Rebecca Grosboll and your kids. Thanks to those of you who listened on the phone: Sue Flint, Ezme Holloway, Diane McCammon, Nola Wood, and Ingrid Wood Springer. Valerie Idusuyi, thank you for your over 20 years of friendship as we competed on the tennis courts and encouraged one another to think big! Thanks to Dr. Hannah Brooks for listening to me read my work to you. You inspired me to persevere. You said, "June, when I listen to you read, you paint pictures with your words."

For those of you on Bible study Zoom: Thank you to Pauline Halm, Rosann Calhoun, Samantha Schrader, Vicky Olivarez, and Gail Wilcox. Thanks to all who contributed to my subtitle search.

To those of you who responded on Facebook: Juli Jass-Ellis, Dianne Kinzer, Susan Reid, Fongie Lanier, Doretta Crawford, Dr. Dayle Woodson, Ekua Blankson-Walker, Pastor Beth Yokley, Julie Vaughn Zara, Paulette Jarvis, Paulette Adams, Victor Moses, Cheryl Weatherspoon, Annette Snyder, Wendy Carter McCalmon, Tammy Finley Oldfather, April Pattie, Lynn Jackson, Pam Bone, La Jean Hawkins, Sandy Daniels, Dr. Cynthia Kudji Sylvester, Dr. Hanna Chookaszian, Carola First, Dustin Bramer, Dr. Joe Henkle, Norma Mehra, Pattie Austin, Linda Friend, Carrie Wieties, Dr. Josiah Zubairu, Lisa Carney, Jackson Wilson, Craig P. Williams, Susan Pennington, Dr. Michael Ashigbi, and Cynthia Shambley . . . I thank you so much.

Thank you to Mark Dedzoe. You were the one who encouraged me to set a date to finish my memoir. You always told me I have so much to share with the world. Francis Yvonne Jackson, your book of verses, *Come Walk With Me-from Guyana to North America* was an inspiration to me. For my prayer warriors, Henry Norris and Sharon Onguti, thanks for your continual prayers for this work.

For those of you who took time out of your busy schedules and read part of or the whole of my manuscript and made suggestions and changes, I would like to express my sincere thank you for your precious sacrifice and time: Steve Seiple, thanks so much! You were the first to read my manuscript, from start to finish! To Polly Danforth, Lucy Dalton-Lackie, John Simpson, and Jared, thank you all for your affirming comments and insightful thoughts and suggestions. Thank you all for lending me your amazing, creative minds. It sure takes a village to do something as rewarding as this.

Kara Shim, thank you for leaping to the rescue to help in the design of my book's front cover. You were immediately up to the task to create a beautiful product. When I needed to create a website, not only did you create it in record time, but you then patiently showed me how to maintain my website for me to engage with my readers. Thank you for capturing the spirit of *Caryl's Closet*. Your enduring energy as you supported my efforts to create a website that reflects the essence of who I am is appreciated. Your creativity is astounding!

To my publishing team: Thank you, Larry Carpenter, for believing in me. The first time I contacted you, your response was so warm and fatherly. You took me under your wing. You answered every question that I had with sincerity and in the spirit of someone who had walked this road many times over. I love your prompt and honest responses day or night. You delivered on every promise. I am so blessed to know that people like you still exist. I would truly recommend Carpenter's Son and Clovercroft Publishing anytime to others. I hope you feel like I do, that this book was meant for your company and me to produce.

Thank you, Suzanne Lawing, for designing my memoir cover and doing the interior editing of my work. To Tiarra Tompkins, thanks for doing a fabulous job as content editor!

To Gail Fallen, thanks for your patience and critical eye for good writing. Yours is one of the hardest jobs!

I will be forever thankful to Ingram Content Group. Your reputation for producing culturally relevant award-winning books is just what *Caryl's Closet* needed.

To my loved one: Edem, thank you for being the "special" sauce in my journey throughout my sojourn in America. We crossed paths designed by God to help us align our future together. I sincerely thank you for all you do to make this effort a success. You have made sacrifices to make this dream come through. You honor my work as if it were your own. Thank you for doing life with me. This is just the beginning. I look forward to writing greater stories together with you.

Finally, to you, my readers: I encourage you to join me at the table. You have a seat right next to me. I know that God sees you. Like me, He wants you to open up your heart and unlock the closets of your lives. I cannot wait to meet with you soon.